CHARACTER AND RELIGION

CHARACTER AND RELIGION

EDWARD LYTTELTON, M.A., B.D.

GYAN

Published by

Gyan Publishing House
5, Ansari Road
Daryaganj, New Delhi-110002
Phone: 011-47034999, 9811692060
E-mail: books@gyanbooks.com

Distribution Network
gyanbooks.com
India, USA, Canada, UK, Australia, France

ISBN: 978-81-212-9400-3 (PB)
First Published, 1912

2nd Impression 2023

Printed at: Gyan Press, Delhi.

CHARACTER AND RELIGION

AUTHOR: EDWARD LYTTELTON

CHARACTER AND RELIGION

EDWARD LYTTELTON, M.A., B.D.

CHARACTER AND RELIGION

BY THE REV. THE HON.

EDWARD LYTTELTON, M.A., B.D.

HEADMASTER OF ETON COLLEGE

AUTHOR OF "THE SERMON ON THE MOUNT," ETC.

"Plutarch has left a tract, kindly and sensible, on 'How a man may recognise his own progress in virtue,' but there is no native Christian product of the kind."
—*Glover*.

NEW YORK CHICAGO

FLEMING H. REVELL COMPANY

MCMXII

Preface

THIS book is an attempt to show that while human character is greatly impoverished and perverted if the graces summed up as Humility be wanting to it, yet it is impossible to see how they can ever have been fostered into vigour and duly recognized in their beauty, except under the influence of strong clear belief in Christ as God, and in His work as a redeeming work, revealing to us the infinite Love of God.

To bring this out certain forms of popular Christianity have been examined, and their inadequacy in respect of the encouragement of Humility noted. In particular the value of the teaching and human example of Christ under any hypothesis other than that of Christianity has been weighed in Appendix A. Brief investigations into the possibility of Humility, as a recognized virtue, being derived from Greek philosophy have been added.

In the chapter entitled "A Year After," I have expatiated into subjects somewhat away from the main theme of the book, into the question whether the claim advanced for "dogmatic" religion can be acceptable to a simple-hearted, *practically*-minded man? Is it not too mystical? Any reader on coming to the conclusion of the other chapters might feel this difficulty, and certainly it is commonly felt nowadays. I have, therefore, dealt with it in a dialogue, and included a further enquiry, whether from the "morality" starting point, hopefulness is possible.

Perhaps a caution is needed. As Humility is taken as a convenient title for the group of such qualities as self-forgetfulness, lack of self-assertiveness, humble estimate of self, it may be found that in one part of the discussion one of these virtues is treated more specially than in another; and that consequently the definition of Humility is not very clear cut. This, which was hardly to be avoided, will not be a disadvantage to the discussion, if it is remembered that the main argument applies in reality to a rather larger area of ethics than that covered by the word Humility, however broadly understood. Such virtues as Hopefulness, Perseverance and Charity might be equally used as illustration of the principle as is here set forth and discussed, though of course the line of argument would not be the same.

In other words, this treatise is a contribution to the question recently come into prominence, how far are we, ordinary people, justified in believing that character can be trained on moral principles alone. My conviction is that all that is noble and satisfying and fruitful in human life is not only God's gift, but lives and grows in proportion as man recognizes that it is His gift. Also that all serious-minded "moralists" are religious, sometimes without knowing it. Writing, then, in support of this conviction, I have tried to isolate one group of good qualities instead of dealing with an indefinite number.

The larger part of the discussion is cast into dialogue form, simply for the purpose of making it less monotonous to the reader. I have tried to avoid the fault of understating adverse arguments, though probably only a few readers will think the attempt successful.

My thanks are due to the Rev. Dr. Illingworth and Canon L. Ragg for kindly reading the manuscript and making suggestions.

E. LYTTELTON.

ETON,
March, 1912.

CONTENTS

(*The numbers refer to pages.*)

CHARACTER AND RELIGION

CHAPTER I

Introduction

THE relation between Religion and Morality is a subject of never-ceasing importance and interest. It is quite certain that there is a close connexion between the two, and while people, in England at least, who wish to make anything of their lives, may be roughly divided into those who set most store by the former, and those who pin their faith on the latter, all combine in exhibiting their own idea of this connexion with a view to justify their preference. Take for instance the view of the Moralists. Broadly speaking and if they are to be judged by their utterances, they would estimate all religious belief by what they discern of its moral outcome. " By their faith ye shall know them " is to them a saying to be so interpreted. Whatever religion is professed by any one, if it issues in good living nothing serious can be said against it : and *per contra* if there is anything unsatisfactory in the life of an orthodox Christian, so far there is evidence, not presumptive, but positive, against the doctrines that he holds. The underlying primciples of this very prevalent way of estimating religious doctrine is that Conduct is all-important, religious belief of secondary value.

But the two departments of human life are there, and neither can be ignored. Hence, then, grows up a natural wish to discern clearly what is the nature of the relation between this all-important matter of Conduct and this intrusive and mysterious subject of Religion. No thinking man can for long acquiesce in a muddled and confused view of the question. If he sets Conduct above everything in human life, he would be glad to make it clear to himself that Religion is merely an accessory, of a somewhat ornamental kind, to the things in life best worth doing. But this, it happens, is not easy to do.

It might be possible for grown-up people to consent, for a long period and over a wide area of the earth's surface, to devote their whole energies to Conduct and the establishing of a right public opinion as to what ought to be done in divers emergencies, but, oddly enough, the resistance to this corporate action comes from an unexpected quarter and is extremely stubborn. It comes from children. Children, as we all agree, have to be trained by their elders, and as the latter are concerned with inducing the little ones to be obedient and law-abiding, they soon discover that something more is necessary to secure this end than the *ipse dixits* of grown-up people, and that the task, incredibly difficult in most cases, is rendered nearly impossible, unless behind the human command there is something of mystery: and that this element of mystery, for which children have a practically universal and almost insatiable appetite, is secured by religious influence, which means religious teaching. This contention is very widely admitted in England, though there are some dissentients. But, wherever it is admitted, the adult moralist is reduced to the humiliating position of having to base the teaching of his child in what he conceives to be the first thing in life, conduct, on something which to him is of quite secondary importance, and beyond anything hard to put into words, viz. religion. In this position there is something grotesque; but the attempts to cut the knot of the difficulty by ignoring religion altogether in the bringing up of a family, cannot be said so far to have been widely successful. The matter is too serious to be tampered with, and while a great many men secure for themselves a temporary freedom from embarrassment by leaving the religious teaching to their wives, the intrusion of the question into the tenor of their lives is not infrequent and causes a good deal of unavowed disquiet.

Hence we may trace the interesting fact that though during the last forty years the gulf between religion and morality may be thought to have widened considerably, there never has been a time when religious questions have excited a deeper or more widespread attention. It is true that scores of men, of undeniable probity and real loftiness of character, flout the demands of religious conformity in a more open way than would have been tolerated by our fathers. It is true also that leaving out of account all who may truly be considered frivolous and shallow-pated, or mere wordlings and hedonists, there are many serious-minded people prepared to maintain that man can subsist on morality alone, who, accordingly, after the question of the children has been somehow shelved, hesitate not to promulgate vigorously a merely moral view of man's deepest obligations, and public opinion in this easy-going tolerant age does not say them nay. None the less we hear that, among the educated classes, if a magazine is to be sure of being sold there must be at least one article in each number dealing with some religious question; and, as far as our observation goes, the report is accurate. That means that a hugely greater number of thoughtful men than could be certified by the evidence of what, they say or what they write, are deeply concerned with religion. The upholders of morality by itself may be and are more outspoken than ever before, but the number of people who listen to them respectfully and then go their way to reflect more carefully than before on religion seems to be increasing every year. Thus, in spite of a vast mass of adverse influences, there is much truth in a saying not unfrequently heard, that the country has never been so religious as it is now.

It may, I think, be taken for granted that this interest in religion is not at all purely speculative, but what we call practical; in other words, men are labouring to discern the connexion between religion and the claims of duty, i.e. of their conduct as citizens. Probably this has been true at all times, since the love of philosophical investigation has never been a characteristic of more than a very small minority of our countrymen. The differences between ourselves and the ancient Romans of Cicero's time are many and great; but it is certain that in this respect we resemble them more than the Greeks of the time of Demosthenes. The practicality of the Romans was far more civic and corporate than ours, and our minds are concerned far more than theirs were with truth. But there is and always has been a certain affinity. Moreover of late years the demand for national self-sacrifice and devotion, in presence of tremendous dangers within and without, has greatly quickened our sense that, come what may, the claims of this present life are urgent and formidable, and impossible, to put aside as trifling or transitory; and that hence we are right in insisting that our religious beliefs, if they are to be justified, must be able to stand the test "how do they work?" Thus, for more reasons than one, the investigation into the points of contact between religion and the practical needs of the hour is more eager than it has ever been; and the eagerness shows no signs of diminishing.

For this reason it would seem to be superfluous to apologize for making one more attempt to explain the nature of the relation between Conduct and Religion. But an additional excuse for dealing with the subject has lately been furnished by the holding of an International Moral Congress with the object of promoting a movement in favour of teaching definite moral principles in schools in a systematic fashion. The object of the leaders of this movement is not anti-religious. They have given sensible reasons for thinking that as the complexity of life increases, duty becomes more difficult to discern, while remaining quite as difficult to do as it ever was. Hence various claims in the matter of conduct have to be explained to the young, and, it is thought, there need be no antagonism between the Moralists and the Religionists. If the latter think that a religious basis is necessary, by all means let them supply it; but as they themselves resort to definite moral instruction in such matters as chastity, truthfulness, patriotism, etc., it would seem that the two great parties are not so widely sundered after all.

There is much in this which seems likely to allay disquiet. None the less, the significance of the movement lies in the fact that, as regards England, it is the first attempt yet made to secure public support for a form of character training in which religion is a negligible quantity. No provision is made for religion; and, in short, the movement bears the appearance of being an attempt for the first time to solve the problem of the children by leaving the religious principles in the training of the young to shift for themselves, while all possible attention is to be paid to conduct. Hitherto we have striven to reach some common understanding as to how to teach religion. It is a new thing if our discussions are in future to be concerned with morality alone.

Yet it hardly admits of a doubt that if, on a large scale, moral training by itself were to produce satisfactory results, there would be a tendency in one party to rejoice, and among the others to think, that something disastrous had happened. As long as there is any such danger, it is clear that the subject requires further investigation. It is an absurdity that good moral results should be thought of with dismay by any one professing any form of Christianity; or that there should be the slightest inclination to belittle those results. On the other hand, is there not something questionable about the assumption, frequently made, that a religious creed may be treated solely as a means of producing the type of conduct which we agree, to some extent, in calling good? For it will be admitted that as soon as this assumption is allowed, the Moralists are perfectly consistent in the policy they have adopted. They have tried religion, so they would aver, in obedience to what seems a universal instinct among children. But because of the discussions produced and of the meagreness of the moral results obtained, they seem to have come to the conclusion that, as a means to an end, religion, may safely be abandoned; not definitely and compulsorily cut out of the programme, but treated as if it could reasonably be permitted to any one who happened to have the taste for it.

But among the questions stirred by this contention is the very grave one whether such an attitude towards religion does not make it impossible to test its power at all, and does not rather indicate a *petitio principii*, since the idea that religion, so far from being indispensable, is only an accessory to life and sometimes useful, is tantamount simply to the conviction that it is untrue. Moreover, if this position is to be considered, it will be necessary to make clear in what sense the word religion is used: that is to say, whether it means pure Theism or Christianity; and in that arguing is involved the doubt whether the latter word means more than the popular interpretation of it, or extends to what may rightly be called the New Testament interpretation of the work of Christ, there being no doubt as to a marked divergence between the two. Such are some of the questions to be considered in the following chapters.

At the same time I am not without the hope that the aim of this inquiry may be seen at once to be strictly uncontroversial, in that it is to substantiate the thesis that the agreement between Moralists and Religionists is in reality fundamental. Often, and I think far too often, the attempt has been made by convinced Christians to show that what they believe to be a truncated and shallow view of life, that of pure morality, must result in an undermining of morality itself and prove to be a sheer deception, a conscientious form of impiety. My opinion is, and I will try to support it, that it would better be described as an unconscious form of piety, that every single postulate made by moralists as the motive principle of their action, not only is borrowed from Christianity, but is meaningless except as an expression of strictly Christian Ethics : that is to say of principles of conduct mainly based on Christian doctrine, which is itself wholly based on the facts reported in the New Testament or otherwise handed down by the Church. To advance arguments in support of this contention will mean a consideration in the first place of some features of the character legitimately called the Christian character, and their correspondence with the character ordinarily called virtuous, or excellent by Moralists.

CHAPTER II

The Essence of Virtue

IT is sometimes said, and quite sincerely, that the famous thirteenth chapter of the first Epistle to the Corinthians contains the essence of virtue. Men range it in their ordinary estimation along with the Sermon on the Mount as an unapproachable statement of that which is a vital ingredient of the highest type of character that we know. Moral training means training up a young unformed character so as to imbue it with the principles stated in this chapter and in the Sermon. If we consider some of the most appealing of the sayings we shall easily discover the central conception of virtue inculcated.

" Charity suffereth long " : this is the beautiful virtue of forbearance. When things go well it is not difficult to feel genially towards our neighbours. But when our lives appear to be in a fair way to be spoilt by adversity and the failure of hopes, and when we know that the upset has been caused by the malignity of a friend, and further when we find that in spite of our self-command and readiness to make allowance, the malignity persists, then if we are able to go on hoping for good, we are showing forbearance. "Charity hopeth all things." To be able to manifest the saving power of hope in goodness in presence of crushing evidence that it is useless; to believe in a fellow-man when it only seems to make him worse; this is a triumph of virtue rare, doubtless, but extolled in proportion as it begins by provoking ridicule. "Charity seeketh not her own"; is free from all taint of selfishness. One of the widest expressions of encomium possible. And so on through the glorious simple words we get a clear picture of that which every right-thinking man approves. Perhaps one detail is apparently omitted; not in reality however. It might be thought possible for a man to be all that St. Paul describes and yet inclined to be keen-sighted and somewhat censorious towards his neighbour. We would add then the great passage in the Sermon about the mote and the beam, and then we must ask what is the dominant secret of the character thus sketched?

It is absence of egoism or what we broadly call Humility. This is a word which is seldom heard in the conversations of worldly-minded people. The ideas it connotes are complex, and the virtue it is supposed to stand for has suffered in ordinary estimation because it is often counterfeited. But a great many men of the world would be astonished if they could realize how immensely they esteem and reverence the qualities which are fairly included in the term.

For in point of fact, as has often been remarked, all wrongdoing, that is, not mistaken action but acting from the wrong motive, is action based on egoism. As soon as ever egoism is discerned, and in proportion as it is discerned, admiration for the character dwindles. A statesman or other public man may do inestimably useful work for the country, and many may be the memorials of him that are ultimately set up; but if his main governing motive is believed all along to have been love of fame, or desire for applause, or merely the satisfaction of his own unusual energy, men subscribe to the memorials and say nothing much in disparagement of their eminent countrymen, but they do not reverence him, nor can they love him. How much more, then, if the motive has been more coarsely selfish? If it is objected that the desire for honour is canonized by Shakespeare in his delineation of his favourite hero Henry V, the answer would be that Henry almost apologizes for his frank recognition and avowal of the motive; and that if he does not, there is much to excuse him in the fact that he is appealing to common instincts of common soldiers before a battle, and it does not do on those occasions to be fastidious about motives for action. Again, it will be remembered that Macaulay notices in the great Chatham a certain want of simplicity, a love of display quite exceptional among really eminent men. But the historian meant and quite truly that Chatham's greatness was extraordinary in that it overcame the foible which in ordinary cases would have been fatal to it. Again, it was said of Bishop Lightfoot that his holiness was singular in one respect. He had no enemies, no detractors; and the reason given was that he was a profoundly humble man. Countless instances might be added. It remains undeniably true that in public life, however useful and however common may be the desire for honour, that is, the approval of the best men, the good opinion of the best historians, and so forth, the manifestation of the motive instantly provokes criticism, and strips the character of all claim to anything so high as reverence.

But if this remark is true of public life, it is more evidently so in private life, in such intercourse of man with man as forms the larger portion of most men's activities.

Scores of illustrations occur to the mind. Self-forgetfulness is a beautiful quality wherever it is noticed, even if it causes waste and injury. It was remarked of a great public speaker that he was so undisciplined in his way of speaking that he lost control of his voice and spoilt a fine organ by misuse. The comment was that X. would not be X. if he could think of such a thing on the platform. This does not mean that an ugly voice is a good thing, or that spoiling a voice is not a pity, but that self-forgetfulness is such an admirable trait in any one that a heavy cost is not too much to pay for it. And true humility includes self-forgetfulness, at least in the sense in which it is here being discussed. Unselfconsciousness is another word for the same thing. It may safely be said that this quality wins not only the highest esteem but the utmost interest from others. It was one secret of Mr. Gladstone's astonishing charm as a personality. To talk to him about himself would have bored him. One felt that it would probably offend him, and as far as I know it was very rarely attempted; but, if it had been, the topic evidently possessed no interest for him. Another great man singular in the same way was Archbishop Temple. In him the trait was generally noted as *simplicity*, a word extremely difficult to define, but certainly connoting the absence of folds in the character which are the result of the egoistic and altruistic motives in conflict. Carlyle, in his essay on Characteristics, notes another symptom of this quality of self-consciousness, its weakness. It is indisputable that, in respect of effective action of any sort, what we roughly call single-mindedness is among the very first essentials to success. But the main point here to be considered is rather its attractiveness, its winsome charm, redolent of the most irresistible qualities in the childlike nature, and able to ensure agreement with Christ's teaching that the Kingdom of Heaven is received as by little children or not at all.

There is much in all this that may be thought platitudinous. But the subject of egoism presents many mysteries of a singularly baffling description. It would be very difficult to explain why, on the one hand, personality is by far the most interesting object of study, no two persons being quite the same, and yet that as soon as a writer or talker takes his own personality as his theme, he achieves the striking combination of being both offensive and dull. There is something downright repulsive in the fact of a man turning his own spiritual being inside out, but if the spectators of this process can by force of habit overcome the feeling of repulsion, nothing remains but boredom. Yet we are told with truth that the study of character, i.e. of personalities, is so interesting as to go far to explain why more than five novels are published in this country every day of the year on an average; and the reason why so many of them deal with the passion of love is that that passion reveals character more effectively and rapidly than any other.[1] Now this being so, one would suppose that any manifestation of personality, even if it left an unpleasant impression behind, could hardly fail to be deeply interesting to readers and hearers. It would be a disclosure of something in its very essence interesting, mysterious, and different from anything else in the universe. Moreover, the information concerning it would come from no second-hand quarter but from the actual owner of the personality, the very person who fulfils the

[1] Suggested by M. Bourzet.

first conditions of winning acceptance for what he has to say. Not only does he presumably know far more than any one else about the subject, but his own interest in it is so powerful that, in spite of a certain etiquette which enjoins reticence, he cannot help talking of it. It seems as if nothing were wanting to guarantee success in obtaining a favourable hearing. But it is not so. An introspective writer must conceal his introspection, or he will not be read.

But we must leave on one side all the fascinating questions which this phenomenon suggests. The observation has only been made to draw attention to a subsidiary fact bearing on what has been said about humility. Humility includes self-forgetfulness, and if a human being offends against the law enjoining self-forgetfulness he becomes to his fellows not only dull—a very curious fact which we need not further discuss here—but repellent. Now, considerations like these entitle us to raise the question in relation to the position and creed of those whom I term moralists. Does not living on moral principles alone, and training the young on them alone, mean that this virtue broadly called Humility has to be included in the creed by which life has to be lived? And will not the training of our children mean a teaching of self-forgetfulness?

The answers must be in the affirmative, because ultimately people, even young people, demand a central principle by the light of which they can walk. Unless a very firm attitude is taken up in regard to egoism, nothing is done or settled at all. No parent could quietly contemplate his son growing up to be a sagacious and zealous town councillor with the motive of securing an encomium in the local newspaper as his only inspiration and stimulus, or entering on a military career with no hope of any kind within him except that of decorations; though this hope is higher than the other, in that the authority which decorates is a constitutional authority to whom the right of decorating has been deliberately given. Or—to put the matter more conclusively—let us consider the matter not in the light of a prospective hope, but in that of a success won. What right-minded man would allow in later life, when the recognition and the applause and the medals and the letters after the name had been all secured, that he had grasped the *summum bonum*, or indeed anything particularly worth having? The nobler the character, the less he cares for such gains. As a young boy Frederick Temple felt elated at the prospect of greatness. But, later, he said that now that it was won he cared nothing for it. Again, when Cicero in middle life wrote his celebrated letter to his friend the historian begging for a panegyric of his consulship, even at the cost if need be of accurate statement, what we feel is not so much indignation at the suggestion, nor pity at the heathenish poverty of idea, but wonder that a man in mature life could be such a simpleton. Our bookshelves groan with testimonies from writers of all ages and countries that fame is a supremely powerful motive in prospect, but when achieved is more like dust and ashes in the hand.

So much then we must assume: that in so far as we are any of us in a position to suggest to others in any way dependent on our counsel, a rule of life, we cannot in honesty pretend that we are giving them anything valuable if we can only suggest the working for fame, whether contemporary or posthumous. So far as that

[1] Ad Fam. v. 12.

part of the subject is concerned, we set ourselves to impart some motive which could be fairly included in the idea of Humility: not anything by itself so antagonistic to Humility as an ordinary ambition; though, with a capacity for inconsistency which has at all times marked humanity, we allow all our words and most of our actions to urge in that one direction, towards Fame, and that one alone.

But we must look a little deeper. In reality, and in all those moments of life when we can fairly claim the attribute of sanity, we require of one another not only humility in the main motive of life, but humility "in the inward parts," that is self-forgetfulness in the ordinary current of the daily thoughts and doings. This reflection leads to something more important than has yet been noticed.

The power and attractiveness of Humility consist in its persuasiveness when it is a deeply rooted quality of the character. It must pervade every thought to be as potent as it has been in a few human lives. That is to say, the question is far more than a matter of a motive for action. It concerns the very central essence of that in another, which we admire. It must be a permanent quality not a stimulus occasionally employed. Though it may satisfy us for a time to believe that the instinct which favours this quality is universal and is implanted in man, we do not know how or under what influence, we are not constituted to be content with this very nebulous creed all through life, nor do we find in training young characters that it supplies a working hypothesis. There may be, and undoubtedly is, a deep instinct which recognizes the beauty of self-forgetfulness, but the tendency to remember self is very deep too; and we must surely be careful to see that in demanding self-forgetfulness of one another as a condition of our love and admiration, we are not asking for bricks without straw.

For the truth is that though self-forgetfulness is generally very attractive, it is not a useful quality. It is compatible with, and seems almost favourable to, a good deal of forgetfulness of others, or at least to that kind of ignorance of what their needs are which leads to a complete blindness to the commonsense ways of satisfying them. Again, it often means forgetfulness of the plain needs of self, and has been the cause of much ruin of health. For these reasons it may easily be conceived as a quality not indispensable to the kind of character which wins success.

In this respect it is like other qualities which we range under the title of Humility. Take, for instance, self-dissatisfaction. Why is the opposite so generally recognized as an unamiable quality, when not only the Greek idea of the perfect man included it, but it seems in many cases to have been a necessary ingredient in the characters of the greatest men in history. A strong case could be made out for the theory that such men as Julius Caesar, Charlemagne, Napoleon, Bismarck, could not have accomplished what they did accomplish had they been forced by dissatisfaction with their own characters to be less positive as to their aims and less certain that their motives were right. Contentment with one's own qualities may not be a lovable trait, but it is apparently necessary to many forms of energy. This fact makes the high estimation of what has been called "divine discontent" all the more remarkable.

Such discontent, too, besides being a solvent of much

useful strength, is not a comfortable fact about any one. It is a perpetual menace to routine—one of the first conditions of comfort to many minds—and it is sure to intrude on our peace just as we are thinking of settling for a time on our lees. Yet it is difficult to conceive of a civilized modern society in which the term self-satisfied would be anything but a reproach, or in which Aristotle's delineation [1] of the great-souled man would be thought attractive.

Lastly, it must be noticed that another fact, one would think, would have told with great force on the high estimation in which Humility is held. We require a good deal of it from each other and we submit to its claims, anyhow ostensibly, ourselves. Yet it is impossible to acknowledge these claims in ordinary social life, even to the extent worldlings insist on them, without a great deal of painful self-conquest. Society requires every one to be at least moderate in talking of himself, but to many people the effort to conform is obviously uncongenial. To many, again, nothing is more acutely disagreeable than to admit themselves ignorant of what has just been spoken of as knowledge common to every educated man. But, if this is done naturally, it excites warm approval, and again the effort to conform, very fitful and insincere though it generally is, is certainly disquieting. Yet we make no effort to alter or criticize the state of opinion which demands this effort. We know somehow that it is right.

It may be taken then as true that though Humility may include some qualities which good men of the world are willing to ignore, yet the greater part of the character-

[1] See Excursus on Influence of Greek Philosophy, p. 229.

istics covered by the word are not only approved of by moralists and others who, without being religious, are sane and sensible men, but are held in actual reverence. It now remains to inquire how far the principles ordinarily professed by moralists and serious-minded men of the world will account for this striking phenomenon.

CHAPTER III

Some of the Plain Man's Principles

BY the expresson "plain man," I mean to denote what we try to conceive of as the average man in matters of fundamental belief. It is more than doubtful if there is any such thing. Beliefs, of course, differ in each individual in untraceable complexity, and a vast number of educated men keep theirs to themselves, so that the assumption that there is, so to speak, a cluster of somewhat similar beliefs somewhere in the centre of a series—which cluster may be taken to be represented by the opinions most frequently expressed in magazine articles, in conversation, in letters to the newspapers, etc.—is an assumption resting on no good evidence. But it is possible, without quarrelling over statistics, to note certain opinions which, whether they be held by the largest number of educated men and women or not, are certainly held by a very large number and are therefore worth discussion. They are opinions which seem to follow easily from certain principles undoubtedly imbedded in many minds and partly to be accounted for by the influence of popular scientific teaching. They are, moreover, such opinions as may be formed and held with very little intellectual effort; and herein is an argument for their being the opinions of a majority of our fellow-countrymen, in whom the appetite for weighing and probing beliefs in abstract subjects is remarkably the reverse of robust.

Opinions of this sort, then, on the greatest subjects connected with morals and religion have to be examined with one object only: viz. to ascertain how far they give a justification for prevailing feelings and thoughts on the subject of virtue, especially that ingredient in virtue which we call Humility. We find that feelings as to the claims of Humility—widely interpreted—are practically universal. If it should appear that there is nothing in the commonly received opinions as to the basis of religious and moral beliefs to justify these feelings, the position we are in becomes interesting and calls for further inquiry.

Now it is often said that the scientific teaching connected with the name of Darwin has profoundly modified our fundamental beliefs in ethics and religion by introducing the theory of evolution or development. It is not improbable that the claim for the degree and permanence of this influence has been exaggerated, but that is not the question now. It cannot be denied that a great many minds respond favourably to the suggestion of the evolution of our deepest ideas on things: that is to say, in a rough and unprecise fashion they conceive of these ideas as having been evolved in the course of centuries by the influence of environment acting on the peculiarly constituted human mind; and the inference from this conception is that the history of each one of our deepest beliefs is the history of a process which might be called natural, and almost mechanical; and that, once admitting that a sentiment or conviction in morals has been evolved, there is no reason to suppose that any further explanation of its existence is required; that it has, in short, been accounted for as fully and as satisfactorily as the mechanism of the human hand. It may be the case that a great many people who hold strong views as to the deep need of humility in character, account to themselves vaguely for their convictions by some such rough and ready reference to evolution.

It may be so; but more probably the number is not very large at present. Indeed, the difficulty in dealing satisfactorily with this question is to gauge the degree in which the mass of our educated countrymen think out the reason for their opinions, and how far those who do think, influence those who do not. Possibly the evolutionary hypothesis has only a slight influence on the matter: that is, a slight *conscious* influence. But it may be true that the law we call evolution has developed the convictions we hold as to the main essence of virtue without our being aware of its working. So that, no matter if the number who would so explain their convictions be large or small, it will be as well to consider if such an explanation is sound.

A moment's reflection will convince any one that it is not.

The evolutionary hypothesis requires that whatever quality has been developed by the action of environment should be, in the majority of cases, useful in the struggle for existence. Hence it is supposed, with some plausibility, that bravery in combat is rated high because all living people are the descendants of those who have been brave enough to survive in the clashing and collision of peoples. But how can any such plea be advanced for our admiration of the virtue of Humility? If the word is interpreted in the wide sense in which it is here used, some thinkers would include in it some few qualities, perhaps, which in a certain sense might be held to be useful in competition. Conceivably the form of self-forgetfulness which allows a man to give his individual attention to some effort of dexterity such as rifle shooting or public speaking, absence of nervousness in short, may be a modern form of the single-mindedness useful in war at the time, say, of Hengist and Horsa. But it is necessary for this theory that not only should the quality be admired, but that it be a hereditary profession, and also the result of training. It may be granted that such a community as the Spartans deliberately trained their youths in habits useful to their existence, and we may allow for the sake of argument that the characters so trained were inherited, most dubious though the admission be. But who ever heard of self-forgetfulness being trained? It is the one quality which cannot be taught, though it is easy to teach its opposite; and parents and teachers have long ago discovered that if you wish a young person to be simple-minded it is fatal to tell him so. To deal with the matter more broadly, it seems quite clear that in all kinds of competition the one quality essential to success is self-assertion. The quality we revere under the guise of humility is, it is true, associated with individuals not with nations, and possibly it might be held that what is supremely attractive in an individual would be fatal if translated into the intercourse of one nation with another. But national qualities are after all the qualities of the individuals in the nation; and the utmost that can be conceded to the objection is that it takes a long time for a quality to begin with individuals and pervade a community. But the concession, besides being trifling in itself, hardly applies to a state of things when nations were small; still less to one when it was a matter of tribe against tribe. For it must be remembered that it is idle to postulate such a process as the evolution of a quality in character without giving it ample time. Suppose the minimum time required is 1,000 years, and it could hardly be less, we are taken back to periods when the virtues required for successful competition were more decidedly those of aggressive self-assertion than perhaps they might appear to be to-day. In other words, we have to imagine the formative influences in the early history of the quality under discussion to have been just those least likely to produce it.

Many other considerations might be brought forward to show how little the evolutionary theory can possibly contribute towards a solution of the immediate question as to the underlying principle of our estimate of Humility; and there is much to be said in opposition to the grossly unphilosophical idea that when once development is postulated as the explanation of a phenomenon—especially a mental or spiritual one—all mystery concerning it disappears. But these matters lie off the main track of our inquiry. It is time now to raise the next question, assuming that what has been said allows us to reject the explanation—thought to be so simple—of evolution.

Obviously if we are unable to believe that Natural Selection accounts for our idea of a certain virtue, we are thrown back upon something more spiritual if we wish to explain it at all. It is, of course, open to any one to hold that no explanation is required. But there are grave objections to acting on that principle, the chief one being that we are bound to remember the educational aspect of this whole inquiry, which has been brought into relief by the attitude of the moralists of to-day.

The claim has been put forward that morality can be taught effectively without religion being treated as its foundation. Those who agree with that contention as well as those who disagree, are bound to think first whether the ordinary ideas of virtue are sound; secondly, if so, upon what, which can be imparted to the young, do they rest; thirdly, if they rest on nothing, can they be imparted at all, and are they worth imparting? My hope is that the further the inquiry is pushed, the more decisive the answer becomes, and the more interesting become the inferences to be drawn.

Our task, therefore, is to consider some spiritual principles which are widely, though often very vaguely, held; and to see if any of them furnish the foundation we are seeking. But, at this stage, it will be well to characterize somewhat more definitely the quality or qualities included under the term Humility.

I am desirous of including as many as may be legitimate, prefacing what there is to be said by the admission that a strict analysis might easily relegate some of the qualities mentioned to some other class. But it is not in any way necessary to be scientifically precise in this classification. Supposing under the term Humility I include some qualities which might more correctly be said to belong to Charity, no harm is done. They equally require explaining, so long as they are allowed to be such as provoke admiration. They may be better described as a cluster of virtues than as a single one. They would include naturally such fundamental qualities as Meekness, Modesty, Considerateness, Mercifulness, Sympathy. Roughly, they may be said to be especially those which were not rated highly, perhaps not observed at all, except occasionally, by the Greeks and Romans, but which have been generally allowed to be the outcome of Christianity, and, more definitely, to have been learnt from some of the most powerful passages in Christ's teaching.

Perhaps a few instances may make the matter clearer. Self-assertion in modern life takes the form not so much of encroaching on our neighbour's rights or spoiling his goods as of trying to induce him to recognize our merits. The humble man does not care about this. To John Keble the praise of other men seems literally to have been painful, no matter how well deserved. Now, in such a case, the feeling would certainly inspire wonder and admiration. It would be felt to be drawn from an intense consciousness of the ideal: whatever he achieved Keble felt that it was nothing compared to what he had aimed at; and when others treated his performance as adequate or excellent, it was to him merely a proof of their insensibility to the higher life. But supposing there had been any indication of "pose" in the saintly man's attitude, at once our admiration for him would have been swallowed up in contempt: what was thought to be admirable would have become grotesque. Why? Because the self-regarding instinct in him would have suddenly been manifested in a peculiarly detestable form, and we would far sooner he had expressed what we should call a natural satisfaction at the commendation of others, than affect to deprecate it in order to win a higher commendation still. We should feel that the former, though tinged with self-love, was genuine; the latter so selfish as to turn a beautiful thing into a sham.

Among instances of effective humility, it was reported of Canon Liddon that he had occasion once to interview a lady on a matter of business and persuade her to a course of action to which she was strongly disinclined.

In doing this it was impossible for him not to indicate clearly that he and others thought she had been acting foolishly. The conversation issued in a triumph for Liddon's "sweetness" of character, gentleness and humility. The lady was all on the defensive, repeatedly implying that the fault rested not with her but with those who were moving in the matter, including, of course, Liddon himself. But by degrees it became clear to her that no amount of asperity on her part made the slightest difference to Liddon's superb courtesy and evident desire to put the matter in a perfectly true light. Again, we see that that effectiveness which depends on a certain winning quality, is really bound up with the absence of egoism. Liddon had abundant excuse for being offended; but as it became evident that he felt no interest in the question whether he himself was right or not, but was intensely occupied only with the truth of the matter in hand, his interlocutor too was gradually lifted into this higher region in which she could instinctively feel controversy had no place. The interview illustrated Lacordaine's words, "La douceur est une force."

Yet as soon as this is clearly stated, a certain misgiving arises in us, suggesting that any virtue which could be indicated by the word "douceur" is only commendable at certain times in the history of a society; in times, that is, of tranquillity. There is, it may be thought, something in it which requires a refined and cloistered atmosphere, when it can count on protection against rude shocks and against haste and stress of all kinds. But in times of war, and indeed of severe competition of any kind, if you once grant that self-defence is allowable you must forego all kinds of self-effacement. Meekly to put up with affronts is to court ruin. In commercial rivalries, for instance, the modern form of warfare, as we have often been reminded lately, we cannot afford to submit to loss ; to " take it lying down " ; but national spirit requires of us to retaliate if we would not perish.

[It would be interesting to probe into the facts of early Christian history to determine how far we in modern England are wandering from the spirit of the words " Blessed are the meek : for they shall inherit the earth." No one can say that the first three centuries were times of untroubled tranquillity for the Christian communities on the Mediterranean seaboard ; and yet something which may be correctly described as " possessing the earth " was undoubtedly in progress between A.D. 33 and 325, and the power of this progress is intimately connected with the meekness and humility shown, for the first time perhaps, by the persecuted and misunderstood Christian societies. A further question of deepest interest would be to what extent and under what conditions would the application of the principles of the Sermon on the Mount be possible between nations, even if we grant that they are possible, though very difficult, between individuals. But such an inquiry would carry us very far afield.]

So plain indeed is this, that as we consider it we are inclined to doubt if after all we have not overstated the case for Humility. May it not be, really, a virtue attractive in tranquil times of advanced civilization, but something of a social luxury which adds to the refinements of life, and oils the wheels of man's intercourse with his fellows in days free from stress and conflict ; something which is quite out of place when competition presses hard on the community, and clouds are low on the political horizon? It will be well, therefore, to consider one or two other instances of the quality, with a view to determining its claim to admiration.

The truth is that there is nothing unfavourable to the growth of humility in an age of conflict and competition, provided that it has passed out of the early stage of arbitrament by the sword. The antagonism between the quality we are considering and the atmosphere of a fighting age is, as already remarked, that no encouragement can be given to the former because at present it is apparently not wanted. For its encouragement, or rather for an atmosphere in which it can show itself, we have to wait for the age of discussion to succeed that of fighting. In the Iliad of Homer, an opportunity for humility is given to Achilles and Agamemnon, as soon as they have recourse to angry discussion in the matter of the captive Briseis. It cannot be said that they took advantage of the opportunity; but if one of the disputants had shown that he was ready to waive all personal feelings, to ignore affronts, as Liddon did, in his eager loyalty to a principle of justice, the effect on his adversary would have been bewildering, like that of the young Englishman's scorn at the offering of a huge bribe made by a claimant to a native sovereignty in India. It was the utterance of a moral *standard* of which the hearer could form no conception except that it was higher than his own; and the native prince left the room dazed and awed at the manifestation of a mystery of the spiritual world. It is hardly possible to conceive the effect on his audience if Achilles had suddenly sunk the claims of self, and in some sense it would have even been a marring of the epic to introduce into it so marked an anachronism.

In this group of qualities, then, there are certain special characteristics. They share with others that of being inimical to what we call our lower natures, in that the exercise of them demands a more or less decisive refusal of our ordinary inclinations. But that which is specially to be predicated of them is that they belong to the gentler side of conduct, not to the virtues which indicate self-assertion; they are remote from any temper which could be called proud. The utilitarian arguments for them are, for the most part, weak, especially in the result, often deplored by social reformers, of the preservation of the unfit members of society. There must be some deep and widely-recognized principle strong enough to maintain the high estimate in which these virtues are regarded, in the face of arguments, far from trivial, now ranged against them. Can this principle be determined? Does it belong to the most commonly professed creed of the "man in the street"?

A brief statement of the creed in question is here desirable. It will be well to include the common view of Christianity on the one hand, with the opinions held, as far as we can tell, by the prevailing type of non-religious man, who is yet zealous and upright in his relations to his fellow-men. The description will be enlarged so as to include many sincere moralists who are practically Agnostics in religion.

We are often told, and I think truly, that such a thing as a downright positive Atheist hardly exists. It would be interesting to examine the statement; but for the present purpose it will be better to put on one side all those who, apparently, are almost entirely self-indulgent in morals, and in religion only conform to prevailing customs from motives of convenience.

The next group which comes within our area of discussion embraces those who make efforts to live up to a standard of morals, and yet ignore religion entirely. Their moral standard would be mainly negative, comprised probably in an eclectic and very simple interpretation of the Ten Commandments with a certain amount of modern etiquette added.

Next would come those who, far more strenuous than the last in matters of moral conduct, that is with a far higher standard not born from convention but from independent thought, yet maintain that their creed, which includes allegiance to conscience, needs no supplementing from the side of dogma. They would admit that they attribute something divine to the phenomenon of conscience, at least to its origin, but they apparently feel only slightly concerned with any inference which they may be invited to draw from this admission. It may be said that to adhere to this opinion means a singular reluctance to look into first principles. Certainly it means a reluctance, but we have no right in England at any rate to call it singular. The position is very commonly held, and among those who hold it may be found strong characters and often a real loftiness of life.

Varying more towards orthodoxy, the next group consists of those whose loyalty to the voice of conscience is no less praiseworthy than that of the last, but they look for a basal principle in the Gospel narrative, or in what they would speak of as Christian teaching. If pressed, they would specify certain portions of the Gospel teaching such as the Sermon on the Mount and the Parables as being the source of illumination to the human conscience. If asked further about any of the chief religious dogmas, they would probably say that they regard them as outside man's ken and not very important; but they would acknowledge that, next to His teaching, the example given by Christ was to them the great inspiration of their lives.

Lastly, we come to those who would be called orthodox in their religious tenets. They hold firmly to every article of the Apostles' Creed, and if asked what difference it made to their conduct in presence of the problems of life, they would answer that the Resurrection, for instance, proved Christ to be divine, and therefore His teaching on conduct must be implicitly received and acted upon.

Such I conceive to be the principles of a great deal of modern religious and moral belief, in so far as they would be professed by those who hold them. It is not to the purpose to inquire how far they are thought out, or metaphysically free from contradiction. Later, we shall have to enquire whether there are not some necessary inferences to be drawn from them, which in ordinary life and by plain people are not drawn, nor indeed apprehended, to the grievous loss of our common life. But the immediate question is how far do they give any warrant for man's unanimous estimate of such virtues as I include broadly under the title Humility, an estimate which indisputably forms the centre of the modern view of Ethics, and is the fundamental postulate of every moralist.

Humility as here used is, in other words, freedom from egoism. The contention is that egoism is a quality deeply and inevitably intertwined with the inmost character of every human being. It is a perversion or exaggeration of an instinct absolutely necessary to the preservation of the race and to growth in mental and spiritual power. The desire to get and to appropriate is at the bottom of all progress. True it may be, and has often been, pointed out that unless egoism is subordinated to altruism, disaster and ruin impend inevitably; but, none the less, the supreme and vital importance of instincts and qualities which may justly be called egoistic, is a truth too palpable to need labouring. We have learnt enough of ourselves to know that, from the first activities of a human infant down to the day of the old man's departure from this life, all acquisition of knowledge, all healthy growth of body, all sound and useful exercise of faculties, all good living, in short, may be described as the outcome of the desire to benefit the Ego, and are certainly accompanied by a pleasure so comely, clean and wholesome, that to make such pleasure the first aim in life seems to us to be not only a natural but an entirely laudable aim. Yet, quite as deep down in our being as the emotions and sensations which indicate this fact, there is the incontrovertible ethical principle that unless egoism is dominated by something else, it not only becomes unlovely but wholly impotent to attain its own end. What is this other thing? Is it given to us, or even suggested, by any of the ethical and religious principles enumerated above?

An answer may be given to a portion of this question at once. Unless the ethical principles are at least Theistic there can be no warrant for rating Humility above Egoism. This statement however is far from carrying conviction at first, and requires some testing.

Perhaps it will clear the ground if we assume a serious-minded believer in Conscience defending his position. He would say "I admit that the monitions of what we call Conscience are supremely mysterious, but those which disallow Egoism are just as imperious as any others and not more mysterious. If therefore I find myself impelled by Conscience not to degrade myself by sins of the flesh, though to a certain extent they seem harmless, nor by perpetually thinking about my superiority to A, B, and C, I obey the monitions as well as I can, but my creed is not to trouble my head further about the origin or history of the organ called Conscience. It seems to me to be a waste of time and to lead to nothing of any use."

Now this defence may seem fairly adequate. But there is a question to be asked which has not yet been cleared up. A very awkward phenomenon concerning conscience is that, if people are to be believed, it varies very seriously in different individuals. I have heard a lady in the train between Dover and London explaining how she had defrauded the Customs at Dover of a considerable sum of money by successful smuggling; and she added triumphantly, "And I don't think it is wrong; my conscience doesn't disturb me in the least." Here we come across a common conception of conscience as if it were a kind of voice within, which gives orders quite independently of reason or experience or reflection, and if they are not obeyed, causes a certain discomfort in the inmost being. But if its admonitions are not justifiable by reason and are not referred to any divine origin they constitute a wholly unintelligible phenomenon.

We may then imagine such a pleader for conscience, whom we will call A, being heckled by a selfish but refined hedonist B, whose views as to virtue differ from those of A. The latter has indulged in some strictures against B for pursuing a purely self-centred life of travel, social intercourse, dabbling in pictures, and occasionally reading, but filling up odd times with golf. What distinguishes him from other people, is a total lack of interest in the characters or concerns of his neighbours, beyond what may be evinced by a casual attention now and then to gossip. B makes rejoinder :—

B. You upbraid me with being self-centred. Why?

A. Because your neighbours have a claim upon you, and your conscience tells you you ought to try to make their lives happier.

B. It does nothing of the kind. My neighbours don't interest me and I dispute your contention that there is any claim in the case. It is an affirmation on your part which you can't support with a tittle of evidence. If neighbours interest you, why on earth is that a reason for their interesting me, any more than my liking golf is a reason why you should like it?

A. But if you only feel an interest in your self, you will suffer the doom of all selfish men, viz. increasing unhappiness as life goes on.

B. I doubt it. Such selfish men as are unhappy, are so because they are perpetually disturbed by doubts whether they have chosen the right way of life. I have no such doubts. But if I had, and if I were what you call unhappy because of my egoism, I cannot see why that should worry you or move you to scold me.

A. Well, but without scolding let me show you how mistaken you are. History shows that all societies of mankind rise or fall according as there is union or disunion among the individuals or the groups who compose them. Now there is no question that union is threatened by such egoistic opinions as yours, and you surely cannot contemplate being a cause of dissension and unhappiness to others.

B. Dissension? Why, if every one thought and acted as I do there would be no such thing as a tiff even. I never have collisions with any one, and you can't point out a single action of mine which has caused any one else unhappiness. Not that I should care a fig if it had, provided that nobody knew it. And, mind you, it is beyond anything difficult to make sure that any of this fussing about poor people and sufferers and so forth really does any good in the long run. It advances civilization I dare say, but civilization is not at all the same thing as happiness. Finally, even if you are right in saying that it has "raised" society so far, that is not the smallest reason why I should bother myself with trying to raise it any further. My creed, in short, is perfectly rational. I know what I like, and I follow it. I dislike quarrelling, and so I leave other people alone, but that is not for their sakes, but for my own. Now your creed is confused with a lot of mystical dogma about higher and lower, claims and conscience, and doesn't appeal to me one bit.

A. Mystical dogma! Why, I have left religion entirely on one side, and you and I have always agreed about this.

B. Very likely. But what I call dogma includes the unsupported affirmations which you try to thrust on me; and by mystical I mean something which no plain man can understand and which evidently has nothing to do with reason.

As with all dialogues, the reader will feel that the case for A might be much better stated. So might the attack of B doubtless. But it is not easy to see what reply to the latter is possible so long as conscience and conscience alone is held to be adequate as a guide of life. The inference seems to be that A is all along drawing upon some instinctive conviction that there is something high and holy in conscience. But any such conviction is borrowed from religion, with which we are so far not concerned. Before passing on, we may notice that the argument is mainly about interest in other people, which is only a very small portion of what any one would call Humility. But the case would be the same if any of the qualities enumerated, such as Mercifulness or Self-forgetfulness, had been directly challenged.

We now pass to a group more avowedly concerned with religion. The loyalty to conscience is, in their case, based on Theism. They would profess a belief that God has endowed man with a mysterious faculty, enabling him not only to shun what is evil but to honour what is good. Hence they revere the character of Christ but hesitate to affirm anything definite as to His divinity. Such affirmation would appear to them to savour too much of "dogma." His teaching they would rate above that of any prophet. They conceive that the Christian law, so given and warranted by conscience, is their guide in life, and vaguely they hope that obedience to it will give them entry to the joys of life everlasting. Meantime all good examples stimulate them; and they have little doubt that their sympathy with what is good is all right and must be acted on zealously. As to the demands made upon them, they are sure they are not impossible and, though frequent failures mark their progress in life, they do not look on sin as a reason for despair, since it does not imply retrogression. In practical life their zeal takes the form of promoting the welfare of others and insisting on reforms in institutions and in customs. Or, it may be, if their temperaments are of a different sort, they believe in conservation of that which is traditional and works well. In either case they admit a strong element of hopefulness into their view of things: they have hope either in pulling up the tares at the cost of some of the wheat, or in preserving the wheat even at the cost of saving many tares.

This view of life and conduct is given, not because it is deep or satisfying, but only because it is common. As in the last case, there is a great deal that might be said against it on the philosophical side, but here we will deal only with the question how far it gives any warrant for the view of virtue which is practically universal among all seriously minded people; viz. that its essence, described negatively, is a freedom from egoism.

As before, then, it will be convenient to cast the argument in a dialogue form. Let the representative of the Theistic moralists be denoted by C, and again the assailant B, who is puzzled more hopelessly by each class of moralist, according as they become more religious. Such arguments as would apply, but have already been used against A, are omitted.

B. I understand then that the cluster of virtues or qualities which you sum up under the title of Humility are to you preferable to all forms of egoism and distinctively the sign of a high and noble character.

C. Certainly. So strong is my feeling on that score that I have no hesitation in saying that the Deity has implanted it in my being. For as you know I am a strong Theist.

B. And do you go on to consider that gratitude is due to the Deity for this gift?

C. Well, no, I can't say that I do. You must understand that I discard all dogma as far as possible—I mean of course affirmations about mysteries which cannot be proved—and the reason why I attribute this gift to God is that there is no other way of accounting for it. Evolution, as I believe you hold, goes a very little way in explaining it; and where evolution fails I bring in the Deity.

B. I see. Where the machine breaks down the Author of the machine steps in and does the work. It may be so. As you know, I never deny these things. But what I am trying to get at is the basis of your belief about Egoism. When you talk of God you mean, I suppose, a Personal God?

C. Yes; though I should hesitate to press the term: I doubt if we can rightly and definitely conceive of an infinite Personality.

B. But you mean that man's personality is so far a guide in the matter that we may suppose it has qualities in common with the divine Personality.

C. Of course; that is spiritually. I bar all anthropomorphism.

B. Very well. Then you conceive of an all-wise and infinitely-loving Person?

C. To be sure. Otherwise I could not use the word God.

B. Then this gift of a moral sense, this preference for Humility over Egoism is something supremely good; because there is no doubt it is hard to acquire and often highly unpleasant to practise.

C. Certainly.

B. How do you know it is supremely good?

C. Why, it works. Society would perish without it.

B. But hold hard. Is not that tantamount to admitting evolution as the explanation? If you are right —which I cannot admit—why bring in the Deity?

C. Ah! well; you have me there. I suppose the utmost I could say would be that the feeling is in me and I can no more help acting on it than I can help breathing.

B. Dear me! A good many gentlemen I could name seem to have surmounted your difficulty. But tell me. Does not your God give man also the gift of reason?

C. No doubt of it.

B. Then is it not rather odd that reason seems to have nothing to say to this unspeakably important conception of the very essence of virtue? Because, so far as we have gone, you have given me no reason whatever for its existence, and indeed because you find it wholly unintelligible, you ascribe its introduction into human life to your God; Whom yet you believe to be supremely rational, the Author of all thought, the embodiment of truth.

C. I admit it is not very satisfactory, this explanation of mine. But can any one give a better?

B. I don't believe they can; that is the reason why I throw this idea of Humility, self-forgetfulness, and the rest, completely overboard. I doubt if it works; that is one thing; and I am sure no one can justify it philosophically. But permit me to point out another serious fact in your creed.

C. Well, go ahead.

B. Have you ever reflected on the theory involved in it of man's position in the Universe? Why, you think of yourself as being evolved by the working of most marvellous laws into a position of dominating the animal world in this planet and gaining more and more control of nature. Why such a being should think himself bound to be humble, I can't imagine. But when he goes on to postulate a God of infinite power and wisdom, the

Eternal Creator of all things, interposing, so to speak, in the even tenor of events and developments to give the wondrous gift of a moral sense to certain individuals, it is hard to see how these individuals are not bound to think very highly of themselves.

C. I see your point. But still there must be a fallacy somewhere. A man who conceives of a God as a Giver of all good things is more likely to be humble than one who does not. Take your own case. What motive for humility have you got?

B. None, my good friend, none; but then I don't act upon it, nor even believe in it. The difference between us is just this. I am as nearly godless as a man can be, and egoism is my whole creed. You bring in a whole lot of notions about a God whose whole concern apparently is to minister to your welfare and exalt your notions of your own importance, and yet you go about saying that self-abasement, or anyhow self-forgetfulness, sympathy for others, readiness to forgive and so on, are of the essence of virtue. You postulate a God to fill up the many lacunae in your philosophy, but omit to notice that your conception of Him must, and does no doubt, minister directly to human pride. In the days when I went to church I used to hear of a man who gave a silly young son of his a grand robe to put on and a fatted calf to eat, when the youngster had only been making a fool of himself on a considerable scale. I dare say his previous experiences as a keeper of swine may have forbidden him to think very highly of himself, but the father's conduct seems likely to have taught him as much conceit as was possible. How much more then if the father were not an ordinary rich man, but the Eternal God, Maker of all things in Heaven and Earth?

C. There is something very unconvincing about all this. Look at our mutual acquaintance G, a believer in God if ever there was one, and certainly a humble man.

B. I grant it. But his conception of God is very different from yours. He goes much further, and adds a whole lot of notions about Christ which if true would possibly alter the whole position and save from gross inconsistency any believer who still maintained the supreme beauty of humility of character. Of course I think G is mistaken and his notions are spun out of man's brain. But as a logical man I see the enormous difference between them and yours.

C. Well, but show me wherein his creed encourages humility better than mine.

B. Pardon me. I think you ought to ask G himself about it, as our present discussion only concerns your creed and its inconsistency with your deepest convictions about virtue. Moreover, let me remind you that you are inclined now to hanker after some ideas about God in the hope of repairing some holes in your own mental equipment. Don't you see that you are still treating yourself as the hub and centre of all things? You can't be easy without some warrant for your convictions about egoism and virtue. At present you have got none. So you cast about for some new presentation of Theism in order to make your spiritual interior more comfortable. Is that your idea of humility? A very common course I admit, but preposterous. You can't make your own needs the one justification for your creed, when the matter in question is self-forgetfulness. How can you forget self by remembering it more than ever, and bending your idea of God wholly to conform to your own spiritual needs?

C. This goes rather too much into philosophy for me. Explain further.

B. What I mean is simply this. I have a friend much to be pitied who, from something wrong in his mind, has got into a thoroughly morbid state. He has everything that the world can give him, friends, income, ability, health, opportunities and a good bringing up; everything except any objectivity in his view of life. As his mind turns in more and more on itself he becomes more unhappy and dyspeptic, a weakness from which he was never wholly free. So his friends are advising him to be actively unselfish in order to cure his trouble. One of them tells him to write a biography of some simple-hearted warrior; another to become the secretary of a hospital, or a schoolmaster. But all of them mean the same absurd thing. Take up, they say to him, the active love of your fellow-creatures as a cure for indigestion; the latter being the result of self-love. But charity when treated as a spiritual pill is a form of self-love, which many people would call profane. Similarly you propose to readjust your view of the Deity simply to give some colour to a kind of instinct which you cannot explain. But this is not self-forgetfulness but the very opposite.

C. What then would you suggest?

B. Ah! that is a very different matter. Let us defer it, if you please, to another occasion.

C. All right. But there is one more question. Hundreds and thousands of Englishmen hold a religious and ethical creed just like mine. They, too, conceive of the essence of virtue very much as I do, as something quite opposed to egoism in all its forms. How do you explain this, if the theory is really so inadequate to furnish a basis for such a prevalent conviction. Whence has the conviction come?

B. That too, with your leave, we will postpone.

We now proceed to the next group of moralists whose religious creed would be ordinarily called orthodox. They affirm their adhesion to all the clauses of the Apostles' Creed, and have found no difficulty in believing the crowning dogma of Christ's Divinity proved, as they generally believe it to be, by the Resurrection. They also profess to worship the Holy Spirit and join in the services of Whitsunday, though with less of whole-hearted zeal than they show at Christmastide. If asked what difference their religious faith makes to their morals, they would say that the Divinity of Christ makes all the difference to the cogency of His teaching. He has given us directions in the Sermon on the Mount and elsewhere for the conduct of life, and of course for a Christian there can be no appeal from His words. In addition to this they would allow that some very stern and terrible words were spoken by Jesus, in spite of His ordinarily showing tenderness towards sinners, and as to the fate of impenitent sinners after death they would feel inclined reverently to draw the veil, but in regard to themselves they would trust vaguely to the Redemption wrought by Christ which, in some way that they do not try to understand, gives them assurance of forgiveness. Broadly, they feel that there is a great deal in the New Testament and in many sermons which, to speak frankly, is to them superfluous and might well be dispensed with, so long as they have the priceless privilege of imitating Christ's example and trying to obey His teaching. Further they would insist that a great many people spin mystical theories about God and Christ which have no bearing on a plain man's life and its problems. So that in a general sense they would sympathize with the last group in preferring a *simple* form of Christianity. If Christ really loved men, as it is plain He did, why should we suppose that He gave them a whole mass of statements which ordinary folk cannot understand?

Such a position as this, or one very like it, is found exemplified in the numerous horde of fairly well-brought-up, serious-minded, upright men, hard at work in professions and constituting what is often called the backbone of the country. Among them, as has been implied, some of the finest examples of integrity, courage, honour and self-devotion to noble causes are to be found.

Some readers would object to the principles professed by this group being questioned at all. The plea would be that where such tenets are sincerely held and loftiness of character results, nothing but harm can be the issue if the foundations of belief are probed. The process must have a disturbing effect and tend to destroy the simplicity of character which is the great strength of the chief votaries of this creed. To this there is a cogent answer to be given. If the peace of mind of certain individuals were all that is at stake, there would be something to be said for letting sleeping dogs lie. But the gravity of the whole discussion is due to the fact that it concerns the nature of the message we intend to hand on to the next generation. If the conception of Christianity and its bearing on conduct, which is now under review, is seriously defective, it is wrong to acquiesce in its being taught far and wide to children. Nor is it to be assumed that the majority of those who hold it are content. If it contradicts the noblest instincts of ordinary men it is doomed, and the sooner the contradiction is exposed the better. Moreover (to anticipate what will appear later), if there are current two different conceptions of the deepest problems in life, and it is agreed that both of them have come directly or indirectly from God, it is puerile to talk fashionable Pragmatism and to make the only test of either of them the question, does it work? There is a very much more vital and more difficult question to be faced, one towards which we are impelled by loyalty to truth and by a desire to pass on to others what we have received, not so much because it benefits them, but because it is God's will and command.

It is to be noticed about the creed now under discussion that, like the two which preceded it, its emphasis lies on duty; but, unlike the others, it gives a willing intellectual assent to certain tremendous affirmations concerning the manifestation of God's power among men, but at the same time draws no particular inferences as to the further beliefs involved in the affirmations. In other words, the creed is not thought out. It seems at first to give a sound warrant to man's deep instinct that before him lie many tough tasks, much renunciation of pleasure, and much resisting of natural inclination. It seems to do this; but what we have to examine now is how far this appearance is true in respect of certain deep convictions, not so much as to duty to be done, as to character required of us. If the conceptions as to the divine working on mankind are limited in the way this statement of faith limits them, they will be found to be not only inadequate to explain our deepest beliefs but inconsistent with them.

In attempting to cast the argument into a dialogue form I would ask the reader to notice that nearly all the broad indictments brought against the previous religious and ethical positions which have been under survey tell against the so-called orthodox position; and some of those now to be brought would have applied to the others, but to avoid repetition have been reserved till now. The interlocutors are B, the same person as we have heard already, and D, an "orthodox" Christian of the type described.

D. I have often wondered how you, B, get along at all comfortably in this world of changing opinions and uncertainties. It is such a blessing to me to feel that, in spite of the difficulty of making one's conduct what it ought to be, I have a warrant in the grand old religion received from our forefathers, which you, I fear, find it impossible to accept. I can't make out how you get along at all.

B. I am afraid I get along in ways which it would rather startle you if I described. If you will pardon me I should prefer to leave my own position alone and look at yours for a few minutes, because it has been borne in upon me since I have known you that there is something deep and essential which is wholly lacking in your religious and ethical creed.

D. "Deep and essential!" What in the world do you mean?

B. Merely this. That what you regard as the very essence of virtue, what, if I may say so, you loyally practise, is something which lies outside your creed as far as I understand your statement of it. I mean that the qualities we sum up under the name Humility are the most difficult of acquisition of any that we ever imagine, and that yet no virtue, as you conceive virtue, can be called the real thing without them.

D. You mean the absence of conceit. But why should any one's religious or ethical creed embrace such an elementary matter as that? Nobody likes a conceited person, and there is an end of it.

B. Not at all. If your creed is what you claim that it is, it surely ought to account for this deep and unassailable conviction in all right-thinking men that a conceited person, one who thinks highly of himself in comparison with his neighbours, is wrong-headed and quite unlovable. Now please attend to this. Your religious creed speaks of wonderful and unimaginable things being done for man by God: the sending into the world of His only Son that He might set an example of a perfect life for us to follow, and utter precepts of conduct which should shape our manner of living, which should in other words enforce the idea of duty and raise it infinitely higher than it had ever been among Greeks or Romans or even Jews. Am I right so far?

D. Quite right. That is just where the ordinary orthodox Christianity is so immeasurably better than the pale nebulous——.

B. Pardon me, pardon me. We are in danger of straying from the point. I wish to ascertain how far Christianity as you conceive of it gives warrant for some ethical principles very commonly held; among them, especially, the very high estimate of Humility. Let us test it in this way. You would say doubtless that it is a highly objectionable trait in a man to be always comparing himself with others.

D. Decidedly.

B. But yet you will notice that the centre of your religion is man's performance of his duty. I mean that whatever you believe, leads up to that, is related to it as a means to an end. To put it quite shortly, the stupendous dogma that Christ was the Son of God affects your personal life. How? Why, by giving a divine sanction to the moral law, so that you may legitimately judge it to be holy, majestic and inviolable.

D. I am not so sure of that. Your way of putting it seems somehow rather to narrow it all down and cheapen it, so to speak. You surely omit the great fact of the divine Example of a perfect life and confine Christianity too much to the teaching.

B. Yes. I was expecting you to say that. But the inclusion of the divine Example in the Christian scheme makes no difference to my criticism. It is only another and more cogent way of increasing the burden of the moral law.

D. I cannot conceive what you mean. Everybody knows the marvellous power of stimulus in a living example of virtue—that is, of course, if it is an attractive example, as Christ's was undoubtedly.

B. I should say that is extremely dubious, considering the way He was treated. But let me put my point by an illustration. You would agree, I suppose, that men do wrong not from ignorance nearly so much as from weakness; in other words, what we call wrongdoing is sinning against the light; not a blunder, but a choice of what is evil knowing it to be evil.

D. Yes, I suppose so.

B. Then mankind may be compared to a man by a roadside trying to lift a huge stone. The task is beyond his strength and he knows it, but after a time a passer-by sees him and urges him with copious exhortation, telling him how very desirable it is that the stone should be lifted and inciting him to spare no effort. What would be the value of the exhortation, even if it were couched in eloquent words?

D. None whatever. I should say it was likely to be supremely irritating in the circumstances described.

B. Suppose, then, the didactic pedestrian goes on his way, and shortly there appears a mighty strong man, some Sandow, who, seeing what is going on, bids the labouring man stand aside and see how easily he with his vast muscles can lift the stone. He does so. What is the effect on the other?

D. Well, clearly, if it does anything it will make him despair at finding some one else so enormously stronger than he is himself. Hitherto he has known himself weak by comparison of his own powers with the task set him. Now he knows it also by comparison between himself and another.

B. That is clearly put; and does it not make plain the abortiveness of Christianity if it consists almost entirely of the teaching and example of Christ?

D. Well, I suppose that is so. Let me see. In the illustration, the effect of the talk of one stronger and of the showing off of the other would be to bring out, first, the desirability of the thing being done, secondly, the fact that it can be done, but not necessarily by the person who is most anxious to do it. True. But what has all this to do with Humility?

B. Well, you notice that at first sight it looks as if it would conduce to Humility in the labouring man. But that is not at all the reason why I put the matter into a figure. I did so to make plain in what sense it is true that the main outcome of the Christian "orthodox" position is that the severity of the moral law is immensely—indeed, infinitely—enhanced by the law having been spoken afresh and ratified afresh, and its provisions greatly amplified by One Whom you people profess to think of and to worship as the Lord Almighty Himself, the Eternal Son of the Eternal Father. Up till then there was a moral law, but it was always possible—and, for Gentiles, inevitable—that it should be conceived of as largely man's creation—only indirectly emanating from God, and affected to a vast extent by mundane influences of all sorts, environment, geographical facts, contact with other peoples and so forth. But when it comes to a definite record of precepts uttered by an adorable Person in a language understood of His hearers and handed down practically unimpaired to us to-day, the case is entirely altered.

D. Well, what then?

B. Does it not follow, then, that the dignity or rather majesty of the moral law not only has been infinitely enhanced, but according to your conception becomes the one dominating fact in human life? It is obviously the paramount claim. Within you is the sacred voice, as you call it, of conscience; without, the wondrous assertion of its innermost rulings, the corroboration of its mandates by the divine Saviour of the world. Now, this being so, there is an excellence towards which man is bound to strive: the excellence of conformity to the law which is hallowed by credentials so august, so infinitely lofty, so irresistibly cogent. Is there not, therefore, in this case, a test of comparative excellence in man? I mean is not each individual worthy of praise exactly in proportion as he does conform to that law?

D. I begin to see what you are at. You mean that humility so far from being encouraged by this state of things is, if anything, discountenanced.

B. Just so. The *summum bonum* for humanity is conformity to certain moral precepts. How far in each case that conformity is a fact can be seen and tested by others. Hence individuals may be ranged in an ascending scale. Everybody knows fairly accurately who is higher than whom. What, then, is to prevent A, B and C from looking down on D, E and F? and where is your warrant for saying that comparisons are odious, or that a self-centred life is a life spoilt?

D. That is a plain question and I think it admits of a plain answer. Humility is plainly taught by Christ in the parable of the Pharisee and the Publican, and in such sayings as "He that humbleth himself shall be exalted," and in the commendation of the childlike nature. I pass over various precepts in the Epistles. Now these sayings and the divine example of humility constitute a claim upon us which would anyhow be irresistible, but is stronger than ever because they correspond with the deepest and best instincts in men's minds on the subject of ethics. What more can any one want? God implanted the instinct and gave the command.

B. That answer requires to be weighed in two parts. First, is it accurate to say God implanted the instinct? In whom? What do you say to the Greek conception of humility? It is a virtue for which they have no name any more than the Romans have? If we judge from Aristotle's famous portrait of his ideal man they had even less of a conception of it. I admit that you will find sayings in the Psalms and prophets which show that among a very select circle of Jews there was some theoretical notion of the thing, but, I fancy, very little practice of it. Barring them, where would you look for your humble men?

D. It would be difficult to find them, no doubt; but it makes no difference. The instinct is in all of us now, and that is all that is necessary to make my answer complete.

B. Is that so indeed? You have not considered, I think, the great stress that is thus thrown on the teaching and example of Christ and its consequences. Remember the exact objection which you have to rebut. It is that as long as your conception of Christianity is mainly legal, you rather give encouragement than not to human conceit. The more tremendous is the claim, the more august its sanctions and undeniable its authority, the greater becomes the justification for X to plume himself on his achievement being better than that of Y. Now your answer comes to this: that a Being of marvellous holiness suddenly appears among mankind. Him you believe to be the Son of God; and He, by teaching and example, enforces with a power previously unimagined, the claims of the moral law. Well, then, apart from other considerations, don't you see that if Christ adds to other commands previously known the new one of Humility, you are in danger of flouting your reason unless you can give some other ground for this command being valid.

D. I don't see that at all. Why should my reason be flouted if I obey the command of One acknowledged to be Divine?

B. Because you would be setting yourself most seriously to fulfil certain injunctions uttered by the Founder of your religion whom you worship as God, principally, so I understand, because His teaching corresponds to the rationally perceived inner law of our being; not because He arbitrarily lays down a law for us to obey, the meaning of which is not rationally perceived at all. In other words, it is incumbent on you if you believe reason to be a divine gift, to bring it to bear on the moral teaching of Christ. To make this clear, tell me first if you agree that there was hardly any clear recognition of the virtue of humility, widely interpreted, among either Greeks or Romans.

D. I don't think you should be very positive about this. How about the stories of Miltiades and Pausanias; and what of Herodotus' comment on the defeat of the Persians, that Heaven usually selects the highest and most overweening among mankind to bring low, and the well-known doctrine of Aeschylus and Sophocles that the surest way to provoke Nemesis was to have the head turned by prosperity?

B. Doubtless as patriotic members of the Polis the Greeks could not tolerate a man behaving with arrogant presumption after meeting with great success. But of course that has little or nothing to do with the spirit of I Corinthians xiii. Similarly a character like Oedipus makes a great figure in literature, not as a warning against pride but because he exemplifies the essentially tragic position of a great man apparently powerful and prosperous but in reality doomed. I think you must admit that all this hardly touches the matter in hand. Give it its full weight, it yet remains true that the sudden and rapid development of the idea of humility and the appearance of the virtue as a characteristic of Christians is a phenomenon of the highest interest in the history of Ethics; further, that the embryonic conception of the quality existing among Greeks and Romans is totally inadequate to explain what happened, or to dispense with the necessity of seeking an adequate explanation.

D. Very well. For the sake of argument, let it be so.

B. The question then comes to be this. If you reject the theory of natural development; if, that is, you recognize a motive power in the direction of humility among Christians, which clearly did not act among the heathen, were the mere preaching and example of Christ sufficient to supply that motive power?

D. Yes, that is our question now.

B. What I affirm is that whoever is disposed to believe that in that teaching and example you have the whole explanation of the results, is assuming that a revolution in human ethics, of the most unlikely kind, is the outcome of a mere fiat of a preacher backed up by consistent practice. In other words that the teaching and example worked a change which cannot be rationally explained; and this is to flout reason. It is also to assume that Christ Himself flouted reason in this one respect, though He apparently observed it carefully in all other respects and frequently urged His followers to do the same.

D. Wait a bit. Why do you say that this change was of a most unlikely kind?

B. Simply because even to conceive of humility as a virtue is uncongenial to ordinary men; and to practise it is to snub all the most universal human instincts. Further, there is a great deal to be said against it on utilitarian grounds by any one who has at heart the development of society.

D. You mean that self-assertion has been a great force in all upward movements of society?

B. Yes; and also that the sentimental consideration for the weak and poverty-stricken, the imbeciles, the morally impotent, and so on, is productive of nothing but harm. But more particularly in respect of individuals, I say that there is a kind of self-conquest in humility which is by far the most difficult of all. Don't misunderstand me. I have no admiration for self-conquest *per se*. Simeon on his pillar is no hero for me, any more than Diogenes in his tub. But, as a matter of difficulty, all that such people went through was a trifle compared to the change effected by such a man as Paul, who succeeded in extirpating from a proud, ambitious nature every single trace of self-seeking. Why, the ordinary belief that ambition is the last infirmity of noble minds is surely a warrant for holding that the conquest of it is the supreme triumph of principle over inclination.

D. I see. You mean that in that day, as being more fundamentally against ordinary human nature than sobriety, purity, temperance, and so forth, the establishment of this virtue among men was a greater achievement than any other.

B. Just so. And more than that. You understand that under the title Humility we are discussing all the feeblenesses and contemptibilities which people ascribe to the self-centred character. For my part I don't agree with them, but I must admit a certain sympathy with their point of view. But, at any rate, it is your point of view, and I wish to insist on the difference which you must recognize between such weaknesses and those which manifest themselves in ordinary vice. There is something objective and simple about such failings as drunkenness, gluttony, avarice, ill-temper, even cruelty. To attack those is to war against something which is, in a way, external to the being of the sinner. But when you come to the introspective, or profoundly cautious, selfish man, you have to deal with folds in the character which only become more intricate the more they are examined, and which, if not examined, cannot be cured.

D. Yes, I suppose that is so. But illustrate your meaning.

B. Well, suppose a man who had been convinced by the Sermon on the Mount that it is wrong to act with a view to men's praise. In every one of his efforts towards anything that is called good the poor fellow distrusts his own motives and the result is not only feebleness, vacillation, ineffectiveness generally, but profound spiritual disquiet. He cannot refuse a game of Bridge to go to a Committee meeting for the relief of suffering, without being haunted by the fear that he is merely doing it because a shallow-pated public approves it.

D. But, my good friend, if he is made miserable by this introspection, of course he will give it up.

B. Easy to say, impossible to do, unless some powerful external interest is aroused which will take the man's thoughts away from himself. His friends suggest this or that. But whatever he tries, it is perpetually vitiated by the question "Is this doing me any good?" Now my point is that there is this most baffling difficulty inherent in this kind of egoism, that it is proof against all kinds of exhortation, even the appeal of a perfect example, because the self-motive is impregnable; the more it is attacked the stronger it grows. But please observe that I am insisting on this not to show the hopelessness of this disease—that is another subject—but to support my contention that between the time of Aristotle and that of I Corinthians xiii. (roughly from 333 B.C. to 57 A.D.) a moral revolution was brought about in the very region of men's being where it seems most inconceivable that it ever should be; and that it is futile to suppose that this could have been done by exhortation and example alone. In short, that your creed is wholly unequal to the task set it: i.e. to suggest an adequate principle for the common modern opinion, or to explain difficult facts in the past.

D. It may be that you are right in saying that the cure for introspection and morbidity of mind lies outside my creed, the orthodox Christianity of to-day; but it lies outside of any religious creed as far as I know. I think too you have confused two different tempers of mind. There is the ambitious temper which craves for glory, and the morbid which is self-conscious. Now Christ preached against the first, but said nothing about the second. I am inclined therefore to concede what you have urged about the second, only remarking that it is a point scored not only against orthodox Christians but against all schools of thought, religious and ethical. By their principles none of them can explain why self-consciousness is such a serious disease, nor can they cure it. But let us not make too much of this; I look on it as a temporary phenomenon due to certain phases of modern thought, and symptomatic, as Seeley once remarked, more of the sickliness of adolescence than of the decadence of old age. But what about ambition?

B. Well, I will try to illustrate what I mean. You and others go about saying that ambition is a bad thing, and I grant that it is decried in the Gospels. But the question is whether a few sayings against it can be fairly supposed to have caused the immeasurable changes of feeling shown by comparing Cicero's famous letter [1] with some passages in Paul's letters, when all the time there are very strong things to be said in favour of ambition

[1] To Lucceius (Fam. v. 12), Cicero begs the historian to praise his action in the civil war more heartily than he is inclined to, and "just a little in excess of the truth" ("amorique nostro plusculum etiam quam concedet veritas largiare").

if it is combined with good taste and a reasonable consideration for others. Now imagine a young man starting life with good abilities and a fair income, untrammelled by any profession and debating how to spend his time. On the one side there is a pleasant programme: a certain amount of travelling, big game in Africa, country house visiting, golf and yachting, or, in the evening, Bridge. If he is pleasant, nobody would upbraid him with wasting a life so spent. But suppose he is keen on securing the applause of his generation, and sees that it can be done by a life lived on the lines of the philanthropic Lord Shaftesbury, even though the penalty to be paid would be a renunciation of pleasure and a questionable monument after death. He will forego all or nearly all of these pleasures to work strenuously and persistently for the bettering of the plight of his fellow men. His whole career will be one of public usefulness and high endeavour, and instead of leaving no trace behind him at the end, he will have wrought changes which bring sunshine into many a darkened dwelling-place and smiles to the tear-furrowed cheeks of scores of mourners. His children will point to what he has done; they will show that where there used to be disease there is now health, a fairly-ordered city-life in place of squalor, misery, and conflict. Why has he done this? Because he rated high the joy of receiving the approval of good men; not the silly shouts of the vulgar, but the verdict of sound-headed, high-minded citizens that he has not lived for nought, but has left a region of the earth's surface a happier place than he found it. Now you will notice that, because of ambition, this person has done a vast amount of good which, without ambition, would have remained undone. That is on the profit side of the account. On the loss side, what? Can you point out any drawback, either to himself or to others which is due to his yielding to a noble ambition?

D. Well, I confess I see none. And yet, there is something puzzling about the matter perhaps.

B. What is puzzling is this. You, like a whole host of other people, give way to an unaccountably irrational feeling when you rate a character absolutely untouched by ambition above one which responds to its noblest stimulus.

D. But do we?

B. Certainly you do when you have the rare chance of observing one. For my part I think the feeling a mistake; I prefer to guide my thoughts and preferences by reason. But if you come across a man in high position who wins the highest distinctions after scorning public opinion for many years, and then shows that he cares not a fig for the honour and glory, there is no doubt you would reverence him far more than another who showed, even discreetly, that he valued the "ribbon to stick in his coat." I understand the feeling, but I try to suppress it, as I cannot explain it. No more, it appears, can you. Don't you see that the more I say in favour of the stimulus of ambition the more difficult it is for you to show why characters quite free from ambition, like that of Christ Himself, are admired? But not only is it more difficult, but also more necessary, if you wish to claim that there is reasonableness in your ethical and religious creed. I give you strong reasons for rating ambition high. All you can answer is that you and the world generally rate the absence of it higher; but when asked to explain *why*, you say nothing at all.

D. I admit I have nothing quite to the point to say. But you don't shake my conviction that the feeling which makes us admire Humility is divinely implanted, and hence when we see the virtue practised to the utmost by saints and the like, we naturally reverence it.

B. Very good. That is exactly the point which I reach always and never can go beyond. If your statement is all that is needed it means that Christianity has little or nothing to do with reason. That is, briefly, why I am not a Christian. Reason is to me far too integral a part of my higher faculties for me to lay it completely on one side in so vital a matter. But there is another of the fundamental convictions which you people seem to share where the inadequacy of your orthodox creed is still more manifest. Perhaps, however, you prefer to postpone this to our next talk, which can be to-morrow.

D. Yes, let us do so.

CHAPTER IV

The Discussion Continued

ON the next day the friends meet again. B begins: You remember my saying yesterday that a man trying to fulfil the precepts of the moral law as expounded in the Gospel is like one by the roadside striving to lift a stone too heavy for him, and that, for the purpose he has in view, both teaching and example are unavailing.

D. Yes. It was to show that these two agencies in the Christian religion are not to be taken as sufficient causes of the growth of humility in a short time, or of the high estimation in which the quality is held.

B. Just so. Now you will observe that the same illustration will serve us in an inquiry as to the basis of hopefulness in the matter of moral progress. You people think a vast deal of this quality of hopefulness. I suppose that in bringing up children on moral lines you would concern yourselves with the planting of the quality, and would consider any character deficient without it.

D. Why, of course. It is one of the things which bring illumination into life. Like a lovely sunbeam on a river. . . .

B. Yes, yes; I quite agree. But on what do you base it?

D. Base it! Why, to be sure, one tells a child not to give in; in fighting temptation or curing a bad habit, if he is not hopeful he has a very poor chance.

B. Very. But are you content to go on telling children to be hopeful when the evidence seems to point pretty steadily in the opposite direction?

D. Why not? They generally act on the advice as far as one can tell.

B. Then let us take the case of boys and girls in their teens. There is no doubt that they have temptations to meet, and they have a very strong consciousness of the moral law. How are you, on your creed, going to give them hope in the moral struggle?

D. Oh well, I should say they are naturally hopeful.

B. Perhaps so. But many of them are naturally greedy. This you try to check because it leads speedily to awkward consequences. But they nearly all are absurdly credulous and unable to weigh evidence, and if you put them in a fair way to outgrow this weakness for the sake of their intellectual health, how can you acquiesce in their being buoyed up for years on a fallacious expectation with regard to their moral health?

D. Fallacious! That word begs the question.

B. I use it because I have been challenging you to show any evidence that moral improvement is within the reach of young human beings, and you fail to do so. I should say old human beings also, only they are not being perpetually exhorted like young people, except perhaps from pulpits, which hardly counts.

D. But, look here, do you mean to say you have never heard of the thing happening? Ridiculous! Young people often, and older ones sometimes, visibly and obviously improve. This fact knocks all your theories on the head.

B. Hold hard a moment. I admit the fact, and I also admit that I can't explain it. But I am not bound to explain it. I am not a schoolmaster or a parson, and so I leave the business of exhortation to those who like it. But if you have any claim to be called a reasonable being, you are bound to explain it. You are constantly exhorting yourself. You belong to a huge organization which exists by and for exhortation—what you call the Church. You pride yourself on your orthodoxy, that is, on holding a certain set of notions about the Divinity of Christ and a Judgment to come, and so on, and so on. Such persons, and all who are like you in their beliefs, are bound to show that all the good advice you give is not sounding brass and a tinkling cymbal. I know you can't; and if you could, here is another consideration hard to meet. You agree, I suppose, that most people have what you call a besetting sin, what I should call a tendency to one sort of undesirable conduct?

D. Yes.

B. And that the faculty or organ within us which resists a temptation is the will, so that a strong-willed man resists where a weak-willed man gives way?

D. Certainly.

B. Now what happens to the will when the individual succumbs to a temptation?

D. It becomes weaker, I suppose.

B. And the temptation?

D. (*uneasily*). It becomes stronger.[1]

B. That is to say, the more you know about the laws of our mental and spiritual being, the less hopeful the prospect becomes. It is like a warfare between two armies consisting of 10,000 men each at first; but after the defeat of one, 1,000 men desert from it to the enemy,

[1] This I am assuming to be the case in sins of the flesh. In others, an increasing predisposition seems not impossible, but cannot be called certain.

so that the second battle is between two forces, one of which is weakened by a loss identical with the gain of the other. Where is the warrant for expecting success at any time for the weaker of the two?

D. After all, you cannot compare a mysterious spiritual struggle with anything so concrete as a battle, though even in the latter case the issues are strangely uncertain. But I should prefer to fall back on the doctrine that God teaches us to pray and gives us help against temptation.

B. As to the first part of your rejoinder, please note that you cannot invalidate the comparison by a mere affirmation. Of course it is not perfectly accurate; but it gives an indication of what must go on, and I don't see what other indication you have by which to go. But as to what you say about prayer, I thought you prided yourself on not having recourse to mysticism. What is this but mysticism. If you really stick to what you have said there is much to say in answer. If not, let us leave it.

D. No; for the sake of argument, at least, I hold to it.

B. Very well. Then of course you are prepared to face the time-honoured bombardment as to the irrationality of prayer. You assume a beneficent and all-powerful God, and then go on to say that He must be asked before He will help. In other words, He prefers to look on at one of His creatures sinking into irretrievable degradation rather than help, if the unfortunate man has never been taught to pray. Prayer for rain or for the cure of disease or the alleviation is to my mind superstition rank enough. But after all, it only impugns the validity of the laws of nature which God established. Your petitions, on the other hand, for spiritual strength are an insult to His character. Of all fatuous utterances that proceeded from the days of the triumph of Science over men's common sense, in the seventies of last century, the most absurd was the contention that it was silly to pray for rain or material benefits, but quite right to ask for spiritual help.

D. H'm, well, suppose we leave that,[1] as I freely confess I have always felt that prayer of any sort is a great difficulty. Why not conceive then, of God helping His creatures in their moral struggles whether they ask for it or not ?

B. Dear me ! a very singular view of an Almighty Deity ! Are we to conceive of Him doling out spiritual strength in a curiously economical fashion and yet with wasteful abundance in some few cases ? Indeed, one may say the doling is nearly all waste. There are thousands of instances of some force of character, some power of will and aspirations after a better life being gradually undermined by vicious indulgence or inordinate contentment with circumstances. If your omniscient God gives without waiting to be asked, He injures the moral fibre of the recipient, as the result abundantly shows, though not in every case. If He does wait to be asked you are no better off. He is still a Being Who acts on caprice.

D. I call this something like quibbling ! The facts are patent. Drunkards do sometimes become sober men ; why they don't always do so, I can't say.

B. You are taking refuge in a rather cheap Agnosticism. But I have no objection to your admission of

[1] As it would break the sequence of the argument here to deal with the difficulties as to prayer—these have been separately dealt with in Excursus iii.

ignorance; my difficulty is that you admit knowledge of certain facts and then suggest an explanation which on being pressed you abandon. Granting the facts, what connexion do you see or imagine between them and God? I have put the dilemma. Why not answer it?

D. Perhaps there is no connexion at all.

B. Perhaps not. But do let me recall you to the question in hand. I say I see no evidence in human life on which you can base your exhortations to young people to cultivate a hopeful temper. Your reply was that your belief in God made it all plain to you, because He gives the necessary spiritual strength. Now you are ready to abandon that explanation *in toto.* You may be quite right, but, don't you see, it leaves your estimate of hopefulness without any bottom to it which you can put into words. You reduce the foundation for it to something purely secular or scientific, and, in short, it comes out, as I said it would, in exactly the same plight as the virtue of Humility. For my part, I believe that many other so-called virtues are just as baseless, but we haven't time to discuss them now.

D. It seems to me that for the sake of intellectual consistency you are prepared to sacrifice a good deal.

B. If I do, I have enough behind, and it is a blessing not to have to pretend. The only thing I understand is a discreetly veiled egoism. I like other people to think well of me, and the only way I can ensure it is by being fairly pleasant to them. But I take care it is well within limits. I think about myself as long as the subject interests me, and then I stop. Forgiveness of others is fortunately seldom required. I molest nobody, and nobody seems to want to molest me. Anyhow they don't.

CHAPTER V

The Rector's Guest

THE disputant who has been called B has brought his interlocutors one by one to the point of being silenced, if not convinced. We have seen how the rational justification for our instinctive feelings in favour of Humility as against Egoism cannot be supplied either by the secular moralist or by either of two typically conventional people, the Theist, or the Christian who looks on the Gospel message mainly as a definition of duty. These persons had also failed to make anything of hope, though B had only challenged the last speaker on this subject, feeling that the others would certainly fail if D failed.

But his victories were Pyrrhic in the sense that they left him face to face with some awkward questions bearing on his own position. He had been somewhat combative perhaps in conversation on the subject of his own consistency and the thoroughness of his own egoism; so none of the others had ventured to assail him directly, but they had contented themselves with halting attempts at self-defence. But none the less B left the last interview with an unquiet misgiving that in spite of his vaunted self-consistency he was really nearly as bad as other people in one important respect. Let us note what his general position was.

B was enough of a thinker to reverence Reason. If his reason did not sanction a particular course of conduct, he thought himself not only justified but actually bound to treat that course of conduct as a perfectly open matter, free that is from any claim on his allegiance. For instance, he had never found any one who could justify him in being hopeful either as to his own future or that of other people, though he admitted that in a small minority of cases there were characters which seemed to him to be improving, if he used the word in a conventional sense. Therefore he did not bother himself to cultivate a hopeful spirit, nor was he able to mind very much if the evidence before him pointed, on the whole, towards a general decline of society. Moreover, on the subject of Egoism he was not disturbed to find that he followed his own inclinations; no one having convinced him that there was any other guide. But he was too discerning not to see that his principle (which in his case worked fairly well, that is, in allowing him to get on in a peaceable fashion with other people) was too insecure to recommend for general adoption. B was a man of tame passions, and naturally of a tactful, considerate temper. It would have been more of a nuisance to him to violate the ordinary canons of society than to obey them. But there were men and women living round the corner in B's country town, whose inclinations were of a less refined type than B's, and far more restive under control. Such was, for example, Mr. P., the veterinary surgeon, whose face made it obvious that drink was his bane, even if a cob which B had recently bought from him did not set the question at rest by stopping automatically at every public-house in the neighbourhood. There was Miss Q., the architect's second daughter, who seemed quite unable to withstand the attractions of any man under forty years of age, no matter what his station in life or education had been ; and finally S, a successful Accountant whose egotism had reached an intolerable pitch, so that the local tea-parties were boycotting him unanimously. Now B felt that he and others who thought like him, were wholly unable to object on principle to the behaviour of such individuals, when once it had become clear that they were egoists as far as was convenient. It was, of course, possible to avoid such people: but B saw plainly that such a line practically committed him to acquiesce in a dismemberment of society; and this he was not prepared to do.

Further, B was a married man and the father of four young children. The eldest, a boy, evinced a very vigorous talent for self-assertion, in spite of his mother's suppressive management, and repeatedly it had been on B's lips to utter some scathing reproof to the young nursery tyrant, when he remembered that he really had no warrant in his own creed for interfering. True, if he could be sure that the reproof would be effectual, he would not stickle at administering it, as it galled him, he must confess, to see the boy bullying his sisters and never failing to get more than his share of lollipops. Nor could he look on at the increasingly vivid evidence of his son's rampant greediness without a growing disquiet of mind. But the difficulty was that his reproofs entirely failed of their effect. They induced Harry to veil his selfishness a little bit, but substantially he gained his point always, and happiness began to disappear from the nursery and the schoolroom. But B had persuaded himself that his misgivings at this state of things were not to be encouraged. They rested on no sound principle. If he followed his own inclinations as to how far it was well to be egoistic, how could he, rationally, interfere with the child? So he adopted the not uncommon device of leaving the problem to his wife, markedly clear though it was that, singlehanded, she was incapable of coping with it. But, at least, B had saved his intellectual consistency. When he was out of doors, alone, it was a relief to be able to say, "After all, the people who live in these villas here have never thought why they do as they do. There isn't one among them who acts on any ethical principle whatever, except those handed down by tradition, nobody knows whence or with what object in view. Yet I cannot help wishing that I could hit upon some principle which was capable of being taught to others. Besides all this matter of egoism, there is hopefulness, and I rather think perseverance also, which I should find it awkward to forego entirely, but which, certainly, I cannot justify so far. If there were only myself to look after, the thing might be pretty simple. I could rub along knowing that the foundations of my creed had never been laid, but when it comes to teaching children—why on earth are children so queer? Yet I cannot help feeling that there was something rather sublime and true about those words 'Except ye be converted, and become as little children, ye cannot enter the kingdom of heaven'. If I could get some points cleared up a little I think it is still possible I might find there is more in Christianity than I thought. But till I do find it, I will stick to my egoism. Nobody can say that is dishonest anyhow."

In this frame of mind B happened to meet the Rector of the country town where he lived, who said he was expecting a very interesting guest for a short visit. It was an elderly acquaintance of his who, as a young man, had done some casual teaching work, but gave it up to give himself time for philosophy and theology, supporting himself meantime by literary work, reviewing for newspapers and manifold odd jobs. He was an old bachelor with very few wants, and as his conversation was a treat to his friends, they often put him up and so he was able to live. Nobody quite knew how he filled up his day, as he spent hours, apparently, in nothing but musing. Whatever he did, it brought him happiness, and it would be difficult to find a more serene and tranquil mind.

B was asked to meet him and at first sight was charmed. The stranger E was short and spare in person, a little over 60 years old but vivacious, not a bit deaf and full of quick sympathy. Under his shaggy white eyebrows his kindly eyes twinkled with humour or seemed gravely intent on some far off thoughts, and B soon found that he had fallen in with a mind very unlike the common run either in that country town or any other. He found no difficulty in getting rapidly to the heart of something interesting.

B. Mr. E, you must have found something to think about in that curious book of Mrs. Eddy's called *Science and Health?*

E. I am afraid I found less to be interested in than to be irritated about.

B. Oh well! of course everybody finds the style very obscure, and that there are a good many contradictions and illogicalities throughout.

E. I could put up with them, without much trouble. But there is something far more serious in the way the book evades the greatest question that has ever been presented to man for his decision.

B. Do you mean the question whether the body really can be cured through the mind? I should have thought——

E. No, pardon me. The question which Mrs. Eddy constantly touches without answering is "What think ye of Christ? Whose Son is He?"

B. You surprise me. It would never have occurred to me to speak of that particular question in such terms. Curiously enough, a week or two ago, I met with two or three men interested in ethics and religion and we had long conversations. But it occurred to me afterwards how slightly, if at all, this question of the Divinity of Christ was broached.

E. And were you dealing with subjects unconnected with Him?

B. No doubt that was the explanation. Our topics were very interesting all the same. You may have heard from our mutual friend the Rector that I am not a Christian, my reason in the main being that I have never heard any doctrine of Christianity which seemed to me to justify the ordinary principles of ethics. One of the disputants to whom I allude is a regular orthodox Christian, but he was totally unable to explain why we, or most of us, hold in high estimation the virtues ranked under the title of Humility. Now I see this inability and others do not. So I content myself with not banning egoism any more than altruism. There really is no reason for preferring one to the other: and when once this is plain, clearly I, and others who see it, have no choice but to throw ourselves on a life of inclination, or else live without any principle at all, which I for one am unable to do.

E. Do I understand that, finding Christianity as you

apprehend it, or, to put it differently, the dogma of the Divinity of Christ, fails, in your judgment, to justify the high estimation in which certain virtues are held, you discard those virtues and give your attention to others ?

B. Certainly ; unless that is, I see reason to hold that any particular virtue has some other foundation ; and then of course I rate it highly.

E. Would you mind giving an illustration ?

B. Well, take considerateness towards others. I can't deny that the practice of this virtue is good up to a certain point. It gives pleasure to me and to others too. But it is plain to me that when it is pushed beyond that point, it lacks warrant and is a mistake. So I practise it just as far as is agreeable to myself. If this is called rank Egoism, then I freely confess myself an Egoist.

E. Do I infer rightly, then, that you would say Christ was mistaken in pushing this virtue too far ?

B. Certainly ; Christ and all other saints, too. You see there really is no evidence that such conduct has ever done any good to any one. To die a martyr's death at thirty-three is obviously bad for the martyr. Who else is benefited ? I am stiffened in my opinion by having examined many of the so-called Christian forms of belief, my conclusion being that those who profess them are unable to bring them to bear on their conduct, and are consequently in the same position as I am ; they practise Humility, etc., just as far as is convenient, and all the time laud a Gospel which goes infinitely further than that. This is a ridiculous position for any one who has a high idea of reason.

E. It is indeed. I am glad to come across any one who is prepared to speak up for Reason. Some defenders of Christianity have been strangely ready to belittle her. But let me look into one matter a little more closely. Egoism means, presumably, one thing to you, and a very different thing to a footpad, or a fraudulent but necessitous solicitor?

B. No doubt. I fully admit that my creed is a very difficult one to preach. Indeed if I were turned loose to reform vain and fashionable society or Bill Sykes of Hounsditch, I should cut a very poor figure.

E. Yes, but you nevertheless uphold our institutions for the discouragement of footpads;—police courts and the like?

B. Of course; because life would otherwise be unpleasant to me and mine. That is all. Civilization on the whole makes for comfort. I fancy I agree pretty well with my orthodox neighbours on this sort of question. Where I differ from them all is in discarding altogether the namby-pamby virtues, sympathy, humility, meekness, and the stuff that is talked about a man losing his life to gain it. I cannot see that any of them really practise these virtues further than to make pleasant conversation at tea and so forth. At any rate I keep myself free from hypocrisy. If I see no reason to believe in this sentimental altruism, I say so and wash my hands of it.

E. This loyalty to reason, then, leads you to object to certain vices—gross sensuality, gluttony, drunkenness, ill-temper and the like, for the one reason which you approve, viz., that they make life unpleasant to you. Whereas in the case of self-assertion, egoism, pride and so on, you feel no such repulsion and therefore let them alone. But you admit that if your neighbour chooses to draw the line lower down or higher up, you have nothing to object. If, for instance, he affirms that a weekly drunken fit, or a certain decorous indulgence of the sexual passion does not disgust him but on the contrary gives him some satisfaction, you are bound by your loyalty to reason to say that he is not only acting innocently but rightly, in accordance with the highest law. Granting his affirmation, are you not bound to exhort him to behave in some such fashion?

B (*uneasily*). I have said that I am of no use at exhortation of any kind: and, besides, if such behaviour disgusts me, I certainly shall not exhort any one to practise it.

E. Possibly not. But don't you see that as egoism forbids you to practise these "vices," so you must in reason concede to your neighbour that his egoism makes the practice of them a duty? Surely you don't mean that the principle you have found so satisfactory in your case is to be debarred from your neighbour?

B. No, I suppose not. But anyhow I could insist, that as far as I and others like me are concerned, he should keep these indulgences entirely out of sight and not in any way obtrude them on our notice.

E. No doubt you could. But did I not understand you to say just now that you congratulated yourself on being free from hypocrisy? On what grounds then do you think yourself justified not only in allowing but in insisting that your neighbour should dissemble? You observe that you approve of certain kinds of behaviour of an egoistic sort, though many people are shocked at them: blatant self-assertion, studied selfishness, refusal to sympathize beyond a certain point, etc. As to these you don't mind letting people know your views and your conduct, and hypocrisy is to you a deadly sin.

But on the other side of the line are the gross vices, and they are on the other side because they disgust you. But on the principle of egoism your neighbour rightly draws the line below these vices, not, as you do, above them. How then can you forbid him the right to avow them openly, when his avowal is nothing but the renunciation of the hypocrisy which you pride yourself on hating?

B. Well, I am afraid I must admit that where disgust comes in I am not very consistent. But at any rate in regard to humility and the like I hope I have made my position plain.

E. Certainly; and as you have been so frank with me I daresay you will not mind my putting a question or two just to see that we thoroughly understand each other. As you interpret humility broadly you would include among its opposites all that we mean by a self-centred conceit, and over-estimation of self?

B. Yes. I don't object to a man's thinking as highly of himself as he likes. He cannot force me to share his estimate.

E. To be sure not. But, though you may differ as to the estimate, you would thoroughly agree that in his crusade against the conventional irrational virtue of humility he should throw off all dissimulation and let his light shine.

B. Yes. Indeed this is exactly what I do myself, while of course refraining from giving offence, because it leads to unpleasantness.

E. Well, let us then imagine a young man who has done good service to his native town in showing how the drainage can be improved. His venture has given him the conviction that he is unquestionably the most useful citizen in the place; but others are languid in this belief, and he finds himself constrained to assert his claims with vigour and persistence. Would you object?

B. Only if he became a bore; which is possible.

E. Then what would be a duty according to your principles of egoism, becomes a blunder if pushed too far?

B. Yes, because it would fail of its object. Self-assertion ceases to become a duty when it only ends in people thinking you a nuisance.

E. I should agree. But if you converted a sufficient number to your views of the primacy of egoism among the virtues, the result would be that we should suppress our annoyance at this person's talk and give him our best attention?

B. Well, it is a state of society that I have not contemplated. But I suppose we should.

E. Then the speaker would be encouraged to go on as long as possible in manifesting his worth as a reformer of drains? For he would clearly be doing no more than his duty in obeying the promptings of egoism; since as you say there is no rational ground for looking on any form of self-suppression as a virtue. So if there is no rational ground, we must allow the drain-man to talk about himself and his pipes as long as ever there is a fragment of hope that we shall be brought to view the matter as he does. But perhaps I may get hold of a clearer illustration. Excuse me asking, but are you a married man and the father of a family?

B. Yes; my eldest is a boy of twelve; and there are two or three younger.

E. Let us then assume that the boy were to write his feelings down in a journal, and that he showed it to you one day, and you found therein a long disquisition on his own claims to be thought a better fellow than any other boy in the school : in short a thoroughly egoistic, self-absorbed outpouring of his deepest thoughts. Now you know there are people who have studied these phenomena, and who tell us that such a propensity as we are imagining is the beginning of insanity, which in nearly all its forms is egoistic. Would you take that view of your own son, or would you on the other hand see in his expressions a satisfactory evidence that he is growing up on rational principles of egoism, there being no other principles to go by ?

B. If you do not mind, I should prefer to postpone further discussion till to-morrow. You have, I readily admit, given me some nuts to crack, and as my object is not to score a victory but to get nearer to the heart of the subject, would you mind my looking in again to-morrow evening ?

E. I shall be delighted to see you. Good-night.

CHAPTER VI

The Key in the Divinity of Christ

THAT night B walked home pondering, and found it difficult to sleep. Being really desirous of intellectual honesty, despite all his talk about egoism, he had developed a faculty for cool inquiry into reasoning and impartial weighing of conclusions even where his *amour propre* had been wounded. This faculty came to his help on the present occasion when he was within a measurable distance of being irritated. He quenched his annoyance by the reflection that if E had silenced him twice it was either because he was a deeper thinker, or else the victim of a fallacy which he, B, would be able to expose.

So he lay in bed pondering. " If I am to be perfectly candid I must admit that this old gentleman makes my position look foolish. But let me review it once more before I give in. There are certain virtues of which nearly everybody thinks highly, and which we have been including under the term Humility. In discussion with an Agnostic or Theist and an ordinary conventional Christian, I can find no sort of warrant in their deepest principles for the belief that these virtues are worthy of honour. It has for years been my conviction that there is no reason for a high estimate either of them or of some others, such as Hope and Perseverance. So I have ruled my life on a basis of pure egoism, as being a principle of undeniable cogency when all else fails : and however faulty it may be in its philosophical foundation it appeals to me and evidently, constantly and powerfully, to a mass of other people. Such predilections as I thought I had imbibed in favour of these virtues I have been engaged in suppressing ; but it is clear that if they won't be suppressed, and I act on them ever so little, all my boasted rational consistency is undone. That this is the case Mr. E has, I fear, shown in two ways. He completely silenced me in the matter of disgust. If X my neighbour chooses to indulge in disgusting vices, I, as an egoist, may insist on his not obtruding them on my notice. But he may say, for all I know quite truly, that they do not disgust him ; if so, I should be insisting on something very near hypocrisy in him, the one sin in my eyes. I should, of course, concede the point as to his perfect right to indulge. Meantime I should pose, as I have often done, as a man free from all cant and dissembling. But, in his case, if I obey my own egoism, I must insist on his dissembling. Now can it be said that that is a satisfactory outcome, or that it has the very faintest claim to be called rational ? Yet, bad as it is, it would be very much worse if the self-indulgent person were my own son. I may adopt, if I please, a *laissez-faire* attitude, with some reservations, towards everybody else ; but towards my Harry ? It is an awful situation, really, to be obliged to insist on a course of conduct for a boy, for which I know I am wholly unable to produce a single sound warrant. Is it possible that Henry Sidgwick was right in saying that unless new facts were discovered, the less human beings thought about moral problems the better ? What new facts are there to be discovered ?

Or, suppose we adopt this prescription and shelve the whole business of ethics; what help would that be to me? Henry Sidgwick was a splendid character: but he had no children. I wonder if this alert-minded Mr. E can give me some clue as to the secret of his own peace of mind. It is evident he has got hold of some principle which I so far have missed. I must see if I can get it out of him?

So the next day B went to find his new acquaintance, thinking as he went over various points in the discussion which they had already had. On finding E he began as follows:—

B. I am afraid, sir, that you got me into a corner twice yesterday evening, and, though it is not pleasant to admit such things, I have not been able to find any satisfactory answer to your arguments. But before abandoning my position, I feel eager to ask if you would be able and willing to give me some idea of the solution of these problems, which, I apprehend, you have succeeded in finding?

E. Nothing would gratify me more. I can't, of course, promise that I can succeed in my attempt, but I can try. Would you mind indicating at what part of the very big subject you would like to begin?

B. Certainly. You remember my position with regard to the virtues of Humility? I can find no sort of foundation for the high estimate generally formed of them. That estimate seems to me, as a matter of history, to have been very suddenly raised between the time of Aristotle and that of St. Paul. The writings of the two men conclusively prove it. The natural inference would seem to be that Christian teachings had something to do with it. But as I insisted with a gentleman called D not long ago, mere teaching, that is not based on reason, is not only arbitrary but is certain to fall into disrepute. Now I remember your dropping a remark about the greatness of the question whether Christ was divine or not. This seemed to indicate some view of Christianity with which I am not very familiar. Do you see any connexion between your remark and my difficulty?

Mr. E, before replying, smiled a very beautiful and deeply tranquil smile; and then said, "Not only is there a connexion between the great Christian fact and your difficulty, but there is in the fact a power of solving that difficulty and all others, if once they are brought fairly into contact with it. This is plain and obvious in the relation between the Incarnation of Christ and the estimate which Christians have come to form of the gentler virtues.

B. You interest me profoundly. But I daresay you will allow me before you go on to explain—to put my logical puzzle succinctly before you, so that you and I may stand at the same view-point in relation to the obstacle in the path. It seems to me desperately hard to get over.

First, we have the mysterious fact of conscience to explain. Certain courses of action approve themselves to us instinctively. On reflection, it is apparent that these are useful to society and by some evolutionary theory may be conceived of as developments. I confess I find it impossible to regard the theory as adequate, but still it works fairly well in relation to our attitude towards murder, theft, slander and the like. But in regard to the gentler virtues, and especially those that are incompatible with egoism, we find that the instinct within us impels us with a deep and powerful emotion not so much towards certain actions as towards a certain temper of mind, and that, too, one which is profoundly antagonistic to all natural dispositions, and, as far as we can see, wholly unconnected with social development, the security of the tribe, cohesion of clans, and so forth. Well, along with this thing we call conscience, is the faculty of reason, a sublime power, as I should call it, distinguishing us from the animals, on which we depend for the ratifying and controlling of the instincts which guide our conduct. That is to say, we do not hold it to be sufficient that an instinct is within us, such as the desire for retaliation; but we bring our reason to bear first on its justification, and secondly on the measure in which it is to be admitted, if it is admitted at all. We all, in short, pay allegiance to reason, and try our best, sooner or later, to let it play freely round these very interesting problems. Now in regard to instincts which are socially unnecessary or even injurious to development, we require, if we are reasonable people, an independent and powerful justification. But *à fortiori* is this the case, when the cultivation of these instincts is always painful; always runs counter to the most universal dispositions of humanity. If, then, we hold to any form of Theism, we must clearly establish some theory which answers the question why the Deity has planted within us a set of instincts which run counter to others even more prevalent, and the fulfilment of which is never unaccompanied by pain. You would probably agree that Theism *per se* is wholly inadequate to explain this deep mystery?

E. Yes, I would certainly agree that that is so. We could perhaps say that some philosophical justification for our estimate of Humility has been elaborated with much ingenuity and some success by various writers, in a way to appeal to philosophically-minded persons. But the fact to be explained is that the estimate of the gentle, unegoistic virtues is deeply characteristic of all classes and conditions of men, and, though the traces of it are faint in pre-Christian literature, the feeling is now firmly imbedded we may say in every heart.

B. That is so. Now is it not certain that when we pass from Theism to Christianity the difficulty of connecting facts with doctrine becomes still more acute? First, how can we find ground for humility in a scheme of things which apparently exalts man more than ever? We are told that God became man and died an agonizing death to redeem mankind from sin. I confess I don't understand how such a death would work redemption from such a thing as sin, nor do I see clear evidence that it has done so. But, however that be, such a scheme of salvation speaks eloquently of the supreme worth of man in the eyes of his Maker. That sort of teaching is no encouragement of humility. There is my first point. Now for the next. We are told that Christ by precept and example enforced the lesson of humility, and hence it is our duty to practise it. But I refuse to do anything of the kind unless the lesson commends itself to my reason. You do nothing to gain my loyal allegiance to an ethical doctrine by insisting that I must obey Christ Who taught it. No matter how effectively He taught it, neither His teaching nor His example constitute any claim on my life unless I recognize, independently of Him, that His message was divinely good, and corresponds to the deepest and best instincts of thoughtful men. Now this is what it fails to do. No doubt the multitude are captivated by such gentleness, patience and kindness as He showed: but He may have been mistaken. He numbers a large number of adherents, I admit: but there are millions who will not accept His sway; and among nominal Christians there is a huge number who in respect of this Humility are thoroughly recalcitrant, though they are mostly too muddled-headed or too disingenuous to own the fact. When I put clearly to myself this dilemma, I am sorely distressed to find that my own emotions still testify that I have not been able to efface all traces of the allegiance to Humility which most people are glad to own. There is the crux. God, we believe, or I suppose we do, gave us the gift of reason. Humility is not rational. Yet Christ gave His life to teach it. How can I help inferring that He was the victim of a delusion, which my God-given faculty enables me to discern, though apparently many others do not?

Mr. E sat quite silent for a good minute, and in his face there gathered that singular far-off look of one

> voyaging through great seas of thought alone.

So striking was his aspect that B could only wait in respectful silence. When he knew more of this remarkable old man, he felt certain that he had been praying during that pause: so intently as to seem quite unconscious of any one's presence in the room. Then E turned to him and said:—

E. Well do I remember the time when almost exactly those difficulties, and many more, were vividly, hauntingly, present to my mind. You may think it strange, but I found in time that they were all due to a grievously restricted and curtailed idea of what God revealed to mankind: in short, that in a natural wish for simplification men have cut down their notion of the Gospel message till they have deprived it of nearly all its saving elements, except for those privileged souls who are so enraptured by the vision of heavenly goodness in Christ that, independently of any thought-out theory, they have been impelled to give themselves in complete self-surrender to Him. They learn the essence of the message, but there are many scores of minds to which they cannot pass it on, or even introduce it.

B. Is it possible that you are going to urge me to study the barren subject of Christian dogma?

E. I daresay that what I have in my thoughts would be correctly so called: but as there are few words which have been so persistently misused and misinterpreted I think we shall do well to avoid that term this evening. I don't believe it will be necessary for me to touch on any subject repellent to any thoughtful man. Speaking quite broadly, the principle on which men have cut down the Divine Revelation may be called the anthropocentric: that is to say the infinity, the supreme and ineffable majesty of the Most High, has been constantly forgotten, just as it was in the time of the Prophet of the Exile, or in that of Isaiah himself; indeed always when any error of magnitude has crept into men's minds.

B. That may be the case. But I am waiting to see how you are going to bring your statement into relation with my difficulties.

E. Well, before doing so, let me explain wherein I conceive you to be beginning your inquiry from the wrong end. You have a faculty—let me say a vigorous faculty, too—of reason. You have assumed that in relation to things divine you may use your reason as the one guiding light necessary for all illumination. But how if it should appear that the function of reason is not to precede the growth of life, but to follow it, and if possible verify it?

B. You use a singular expression there: "the growth of life": but my subject is the acquisition of truth, surely a very different thing. I am aware that a human being cannot physically grow by first thinking how he will do it; indeed, if he were to try he might hinder his growth. But what has that to do with the growth of intelligence, which of course is a rational matter?

E. Have you any right to assume that the laws of spiritual growth are so very different from those of physical growth? Do you assent to Herbert Spencer's celebrated dictum: "All knowledge is a verification of assumptions"? "All knowledge," he says; if he is right, then, the attempt to satisfy the reason, however good at a later stage, must be nothing but an impediment at first; if it leads us to hold our as yet unproved assumptions too cheaply.

B. Dear me! Can that be true? I know of course that the greatest discoveries in science have often been exactly of that nature. Darwin had an idea of Natural Selection, not after, but before he collected the vast store of evidence in its support. But, to keep close to the matter in hand, how does that justify one in valuing Humility merely because Christ preached it?

E. It is possible to present a new view of things to the heart before the head. If this is successfully done, there is a sort of embracing the idea by the whole being of a man followed by all manner of rich and unexpected verification by the reason, or what we call the head. You would agree no doubt that in many cases of advance in real knowledge, something emotional or something concerned with the affections is always enlisted early, otherwise the necessary assimilative effort cannot be made.

B. Yes, I should not demur to that, though it is expressed perhaps a little strongly.

E. Perhaps. But that will hardly matter when we reflect that this axiom, if it is ever true, is the more certain to be so the higher the truth with which we are concerned. I mean that a great, high truth demands all our faculties and appeals to the whole of our being. In respect of such a wondrous subject as our relation to God our Creator, it is hardly conceivable that so vital, so integral a part of our being as our affections can be left out. Very well then. Granting this, and remembering that it is no disparagement to our reason to define its function truly, instead of making fictitious claims for it, we may proceed to the question how our deep and universal instinct, in favour of the gentler virtues and adverse to what we call egoism, is justified.

Let us set before us the alternatives. Between 330 B.C. and 57 A.D. this marvellous development in ethical thought is observable. You and I agree that as St. Paul is obviously responsible to a large extent for the change, there must have been experiences in his life which go far to explain how his mind was affected. Now before his conversion should you say that we can see evidences of a propensity towards Humility such as would make a profound change of opinion and feeling in him a probable event?

B. No. I cannot honestly say we do. The description of Saul at the time of the death of Stephen is not that of a man inclined to be humble.

E. Then it becomes more difficult than ever to ascribe the change simply to the influence of Christ's example.

For St. Paul's case differs from that of the other Apostles in one striking respect. He had not, as far as we know, any first-hand knowledge of Jesus of Nazareth; that is of Christ in His humiliation. It is most remarkable how in his writings he never refers to any of His doings on earth, and scarcely ever to His teaching. Now if either Christ's example or His teaching had been the influence to which the great change in Saul's mind is to be attributed, it is inconceivable that both should be excluded from the letters in which he lays bare his inmost thoughts and his deepest principles of conduct and spiritual life.[1]

B. (as if to himself). There is certainly something in that. The great chapter in the Corinthians about Charity appeals to every right-hearted man and woman, not only as one of the noblest things ever written, but as one of the simplest. If Saul was plainly indisposed towards humility before his conversion, yet in later years not only exhibited the virtue most completely, but explained it in matchless style, the change cannot be ascribed to nothing: nor to Christ's example, which he had not witnessed and very rarely mentions. No. I admit the mere example of conduct cannot have been the cause in Saul's case. But must we not recognize an enormous difference between the example of Christ and that of others? If this is so, may we not suppose that His example did influence many minds and brought about a change of feeling which must have influenced even Saul in time? I mean that in Christ's brief public life there were manifested the most superb powers; for whether we believe the miracles or not, it is certain they were imputed to Him. The whole picture is that of One Who held the

[1] This statement seems to ignore Phil. ii. 7, but see below.

people in the hollow of His hand, but Who, from principle, discarded all idea of earthly triumph, as well as all rewards which the world could give, and underwent shame, disrepute, homelessness, agony and martyrdom. It seems to me little short of absurd to suppose such behaviour to have had no effect on mankind.

E. First I would answer that even if your statement and inference are beyond criticism in their main outlines, you leave unexplained the effect on St. Paul's own character. If the example was so surpassingly striking and potent as you describe, and worked in the direction you imagine, it remains quite inexplicable that the Apostle referred to it so seldom: and further that in the famous passage Philippians ii. 7, which seems to be an exception, it is not Christ's *conduct* which is alluded to, but the divine action which we call the Incarnation. Still further: I must demur, not to the statement you have just made, but to the theory that Christ, viewed as mere man, exhibited the virtue which we call Humility. Interspersed among His sayings there are words which, on the human theory, have ever been regarded as advancing the most preposterous claims: and there are certain actions, such as the cleansing of the Temple, which are incompatible with our idea of Humility nowadays. I say this because I am trying to view the facts from your position; that of one who considers Jesus to have been merely man.

B. I am not sure, but are not most of those sayings in the Fourth Gospel, which I presume we cannot treat as evidence?

E. Many of them are in the Synoptic Gospels; and even if they were not, and even if the Fourth Gospel were not written by St. John, you have to explain why some early disciple or pupil of a disciple not only attributed such sayings to Jesus, but found a wide and warm welcome for his narrative. If Jesus were, as you say, pre-eminently humble, in our sense of the word, how do you explain the acceptance by the next generation of a narrative which ascribes to Him such a saying as "I and the Father are one"?

B. I confess I never thought of that.

E. You see there is, as every one admits, a large mystical element in the discourses contained in the Fourth Gospel. Sundry critics, biased possibly in favour of the human view of Christ, have tried to show that those discourses were not authentic: but written by some one who never heard Him speak. But the more fictitious the sayings are, and the more discrepant from Christ's ordinary talk, the more difficult it is to account for such narratives being looked on as congruous to the true tradition of His sayings.

B. Then why were they received?

E. Because they were not discrepant from the true tradition. Indeed, there are quite enough claims of a superhuman kind embodied in the Synoptic records, and attributed to Christ, to make one infer that though He preached self-abasement in words of matchless power, He never spoke of Himself at all in the tone universal among the most saintlike of His followers. In other words, unless you concede the dogma of His divinity you must admit that His example of humility comes to very little: it is, in short, the example of One Who preached humility to others, but Himself said and did things far from humble.

B. If that is true, how do you explain that His character is generally thought to be adorable?

E. I hope to touch on that question later. Meantime pardon me if I keep strictly to the question of the power of Christ's example in this one virtue. As a last objection to your suggestion of the peculiar potency of that example, let me point out that if mere example could work a change in men's minds and ideas, we should have found that other examples prior to Christianity had done so; such as those of the Jewish prophets, and, among the Greeks, besides Socrates, that of Aristides perhaps, though it is true that along with almost total absence of precepts of humility in Greece we find apparently very little practice of it. In short, we are not entitled to ascribe the marvellous change which certainly came about in ethics after the foundation of Christianity to the mere example of Christ, when, apart from other reasons, there had been anticipations of that example which ought to have yielded fruit proportionate to their power, but which as a fact yielded none.

B. I have often thought about this subject before; but, I must say, there is something in the way you put it which suggests to me not only new notions but new difficulties. Once again, then, I would ask of your kindness if you would consent to another adjournment of our debate, as I wish to resume it after a little thought.

E. Please make no apology for claiming some of my time. Among the many forms of activity which a Christian may choose there are two forms of discussion; one the most barren and repulsive form of human effort; the other not only fruitful, but in every way and at every stage delightful. The first is controversy with a man determined to preserve his own limitations who, while preserving his own, makes you stiffen yours; the other, a real inquiry into truth along with one who knows that all human horizons fade into mystery, a discussion which brings new light to the answerer even more than to the questioner. I assure you I feel myself in your debt.

B. Thank you. I will go now, and come back to-morrow morning.

B went away pondering as before. He was somewhat bewildered at the turn the exposition had just taken. For years he had argued with so-called Christians that the example of Christ gave no warrant for our conception of Humility: but E's words seemed to him to pierce deep into some preconceptions of his own which it was uncomfortable to disturb. If Christ's bare example of humility was so powerless to effect the change, so dubious indeed as a pattern before men, what about other virtues? He had generally taken it for granted that Christ's example had taught men love for others, social service, kindness to children, temperance, fortitude and so on; and that though men who worship Him as Divine perhaps see more in the example than an Agnostic, yet any right-minded man must be kindled to some extent in his soul by the story of the Passion; in no other way could he account for the almost unstinted admiration with which Socinians, Jews, materialists even, regarded Him, and which made them assent to the verdict even of His enemies that He was sinless; "Why what evil hath He done?" "I have betrayed the innocent blood," and so on. But if E is right (thought B) we have been resting far too much on the power of example; and this is true with respect to virtues other than Humility; at least I think so, if he is right. I must tackle him on this question, which is no light or impertinent one.

The next day B found E, as before, alert, courteous and acute, but better than all these, full of ideas, and eager to impart them.

B. On thinking over what you said yesterday I have been puzzled by this difficulty. Hitherto I have always thought that ordinary virtues, by which I mean obviously useful virtues, were recognized by men as exhibited by Christ, but that Humility was an exception in being a virtue without use, and so difficult to justify or understand that, to an inquirer like myself, Christ's example was not enough to give it the needed warrant. But from something you said I should gather that you would include other virtues in this description, and be inclined to ascribe the *general* improvement in ethics, consequent on Christianity, to something different from example or teaching. If you exclude Christ's example from the category of the influences which effected this improvement, not only do you utter a strange paradox, but *à fortiori* you exclude also the examples of holy men like Paul, Ignatius and a host of others.

E. I am glad you have touched on this side of the matter. To deal with it means to depart for a time from the exact question before us, the warrant for a high estimate of Humility, into an inquiry into the place of Christ's example in reference to all the specifically Christian virtues, faith, hope, charity, etc. About them all I would say with conviction that you get no warrant for any one of them from contemplating the story of Christ, unless you have consciously or unconsciously in your mind the presupposition that He was divine, and came on earth to die for our sins.

B. You amaze me! Please explain.

E. Take the most obvious characteristic of Christ's

conduct, His heroic fortitude during the Passion, or the calm strength with which He saw the forces of His adversaries closing around Him, with the grim certainty of His approach to an agonizing death. Does this conduct inspire us to heroism or does it not? The answer to that question depends on what you conceive to have been the object in view throughout. If there was no object, the heroism becomes fanaticism, and it is easy to see that, on the purely human hypothesis, the public life of Christ is open to an unanswerable indictment.

B. How so? I am not clear as to the distinction, though of course there is one, between heroism and fanaticism.

E. Is it not this, that the ardour, the unconquerable fortitude, the self-forgetfulness and triumphant faith of the hero, becomes something not far removed from insanity when the main object of it all is suspected of being a delusion? If it be a palpable and ludicrous delusion the hero becomes a sheer lunatic: but if it be merely inadequate or partial, we dub him a fanatic. The hero endures all things, conquers all opposition, sees a meaning in all disappointments, because his eyes are set on something universally recognized as eternal and good. Now take away the purpose of Christ's earthly career which the dogma of divinity allows us to discern, and I maintain that what is left is not a noble human example at all, but a series of actions far too fragmentary to be useful for imitation and far too aimless to be admired.

B. Good gracious! I can make nothing of this. Do you deny Him courage, for instance?

E. Courage, my dear sir, ceases to be a virtue if it is merely a facing of horrors for an unworthy object or for no object at all. The reason why Don Quixote's charging of the windmill is not heroism, is that the windmill was a windmill and not what he supposed it to be. Now it is becoming increasingly difficult for me to imagine clearly what Christ was, if He was only human: what His career really was, if we strip it of the glamour thrown over it by the presupposition that He was in some sense divine, and therefore that, however difficult to interpret, His story was unutterably noble and His example supremely inspiring. But I am speaking simple truth when I say that to any one really convinced that Christ was mere man, His actions and His teaching become wholly useless as a guide to good living, and wholly unintelligible. We must treat it with the respect which anything momentous claims of us, and look for its purpose. Why, on that theory, did Christ die? It is patent to any reader of the Gospels that He need not have died, and I say that His death was either the Redemption of mankind from Sin, or a useless suicide. Is it suggested that the heroism of it consisted in the unflinching courage with which He faced pain? Then I answer that many a lunatic has slain himself by rushing on death without the faintest symptom of hesitation, but the more unhesitating the self-sacrifice is, the madder it is, unless you can discern a purpose which it goes far to attain, or a principle which it helps to interpret.

B. Well, but surely the good of mankind is a principle of conduct worthy enough. Common-sense is against you. The Death of Christ has ever been spoken of as a tragedy in which all the hope of the human race is stored. It has done wonders for the softening of civilization, and in teaching us that true spiritual influence depends in some degree upon death. If the blood of the martyrs was the seal of the Church, it was because they imitated Christ in their deaths. Similarly a man who disbelieves in His divinity, can imitate His self-surrender and His courage.

E. What! even without attempting to discern a purpose in it all? I venture to say that of all those who really admire Christ's teaching and career, there is not one who does not postulate to himself that the purpose of His life was in some sense a bringing of man nearer to God. Think of this. If His teaching and example were everything, why did He cut them short by dying in the prime of His early manhood? You will surely admit that any great man is great because he overcomes obstacles in pressing towards a worthy goal, a "prize of his high calling"; the grand characteristic of greatness is that it knows its own aim, and in the midst of all the will o' the wisps of this deceptive world it holds on its way steadily, and interprets the purpose of life with a clearness and consistency which, after some time, future generations are able to discern, to honour, and in this case to adore. Now grasp firmly the postulate of the many modern self-styled Christians who put their whole trust in a merely human Christ. It comes to this, that the whole significance of Christ's work lies not in His Sacrifice, because that was merely the death of a strong man Who opposed the spirit of His age, nor in His miracles, because they are thought to be historically doubtful, nor in His Resurrection because, besides being deemed doubtful, it cannot be of use for imitation; but that it lies solely in His teaching and moral example. Is not that so?

B. Yes, I would not dispute that.

E. Very well. Reflect now on the way in which the

hero fulfilled his part in the world. If teaching is to be of real use it must be heard or read. Jesus of Nazareth took no pains to secure either one or the other. He never gave any directions for the preservation of His discourses, and the result is that we only have fragmentary accounts of them, varying in their wording. Again, He evidently shrank more and more from such publicity as He tolerated at first, and which alone gave any reasonable prospect of His precepts obtaining a wide vogue. Again, a most fatal objection to His teaching is that it possessed a certain charm, very difficult to define, which except on the divine hypothesis comes to very little more than charm, because the teaching was so metaphorical and paradoxical as to be useless as practical precepts for guidance to men in perplexities: and that is true, even where the words are not dealing with mysteries which a modern Socinian quite rightly disregards, but with practical everyday matters such as the treatment of beggars in the street, the reception of affronts, the explosion of a hot temper and the saving against old age. Once more, even if a loyal reader can find edification in these very baffling paragraphs, he must admit that they profess to touch hardly one of the really pressing questions of this or any other age. Now you may say what you please as to the beauty of a man's phraseology and illustrations, and the wisdom of his instructions, but you must in all honesty confess it to be disappointing, when, in ninety-nine out of every hundred of the pressing difficulties of practical life, you may turn to his teaching and find not a single hint: and in the hundredth it is more likely than not that the injunction will be a vivid paradox wholly impossible to carry out in this or any period of human history.

B. Very well. Supposing now for the sake of argument that the divine hypothesis is necessary to explain the excellence of the effect upon mankind of Christ's work, why not believe that it was a delusion permitted by God? I suppose you and every thoughtful reader of the Old Testament agree that there was a time when the slaughter of tribal enemies was universally held to be an act of duty, and now we equally agree that the verses in the Psalms which pungently express that sentiment are out of harmony with modern ideas. In short the conception of duty has changed; that is, according to your creed, God has told men different things at different times. If this is accepted in morals, why is it thought to be impious to suggest that God may have permitted the human race to have conceived wrongly about Christ, when the mistake has been productive of great good?

E. Because the two things are not in the same plane. Consider a child whose whole inspiration of life comes from the sense of his parents' deep and unchangeable love for him, which is the normal condition of a healthy-minded child. Now that sense is based on the evidence of many loving acts, and its growth is an outcome of trust. But supposing it were possible for a parent to arrange so that the loving acts were only loving in appearance, being in reality not evidences of love at all; but that he did them knowing they would be misunderstood, but beneficially and usefully, by the child; and yet that after a few years it was quite certain that they would be understood in their true nature as quite indifferent. Such an education would be a hollow pretence, subversive of all trust, all harmony and love, and, in the deepest things of life, the child would be taught to despair of truth.

B. Yes, but what about the changing of the moral conceptions?

E. That is merely the working of a natural law. We know, all of us, that as the virtue of a child is not the same as that of an adult, so the rules of conduct obeyed by a child are outgrown by the man. There is nothing in this but recognition of a fundamental law of growth. But for the parent to play fast and loose with that which is the very centre and mainspring of the child's moral and spiritual health is to make all permanent relation between the two impossible. Translate this into terms suitable to the matter in hand. Christ told His followers to be childlike. What could be less childlike than to conceive of a Father Who for centuries teaches His children in the very inmost shrine of thought and feeling to nourish a conviction about Himself which rests on nothing? Not about the mysteriousness of His Being, but the simple vital conviction that He loves us? Hence we must subtract from Christ's teaching all the injunctions as to child-likeness. What are we to make of the remainder? If God taught our fathers to base their whole view of life upon so vast and all pervading a delusion as that which imagines the Incarnation and Redemption of the world and the victory over Death and Sin, is there not a presumption that our modern view of His teaching is as baseless as theirs was, though it be for the time useful? Why not, then, treat it as binding on us only when it humours our inclinations? As soon as He tells us anything we did not know before, we had better ignore it. Indeed as soon as the teaching is felt to be really inspiring, we ought to suspect it of being based on falsehood. Now I ask what have the men of our day done to deserve this tremendous penalty?

We have been led to find out, have we? that resolute and conscientious inquiry leads to the shattering of the whole fabric of hope and joy built up by men who own their whole knowledge of it to be based on Christ's work: that obedience to our reason deprives us of all assurance of God's Fatherhood, and turns the one guarantee that Creation is not a failure into a hollow deception. What have we done to deserve this reward of careful thinking?

B. (*after a pause*). Well, let us put on one side the delusion-hypothesis. How, then, would you deal with the difficulties of the case, on the hypothesis that Christ's divinity was a fact?

E. Stay a moment. I want to deal with the remaining half of His work—His moral example. The more you regard it as simply a pattern for imitation the more useless it becomes. How can we living in England to-day, with lives conditioned in 10,000 different ways, follow the outward example of an itinerant preacher in a remote country 2,000 years ago? What was that example? It was that of a Man Who taught! But are all Christians to set about teaching? He went about healing. But are we all to do the same? Suppose we can't heal, what then? There is only one department of His life which could possibly be imitated literally by a modern follower, and that is His practice of prayer. But you will observe, unless you hold a lot of theories which are outside of and beyond the human hypothesis, that it must be admitted there is no evidence that His prayers were any more *useful* than other people's: and, without the presuppositions, remember that usefulness to man is the one and only test of value. Moreover, it simplifies the discussion, if we note that this particular department of Christ's conduct, that in which He may be imitated, His followers who think of Him as merely human have quietly ignored. I mean that, without libelling them, one may say that they are not distinguished for any fervent belief in, or practice of, prayer.

B. Well what do you say to this? I remember reading in years gone by in the *Church Quarterly* an article which contended that Christ's example was useless not for the reasons you give, but because it was unapproachably sublime. Now is it conceivable that the same Man can be truly spoken of in such very different tones?

E. Anything in this way is conceivable if we remember man's almost infinite power of holding contradictory theories together in his mind. The volume of belief in His divinity which has gathered force throughout the nineteen centuries makes it difficult for the quickest-witted pamphleteers and lecturers to divest themselves wholly of the beliefs in which they were brought up, and which are still permeating the atmosphere round them. Doubtless an immense majority of European Christians find it easier to contemplate the outward aspect of Christ's story, since a continuous and exacting effort is required to keep hold of the conception of the Incarnation and Redemption throughout. We all of us constantly fall back exhausted on to the moral conception, thinking we have abandoned the other. But we have not. We are far too muddle-headed to notice it, but under our appreciation of Christ's example is an assumption that He was something ineffably great.

B. This is still very strange to me. Let us take an example. One of the most winning and gracious things He ever did was the blessing of the little children, coupled with the immortal words that He spoke then. Am I to be debarred from admiring that unless I hold to the Nicene Creed?

E. You could hardly have chosen a better example. It was indeed a gracious action if the Son of God spoke and acted so towards the little barefooted peasant children of that out of the way land. But if He were merely an itinerant peasant teacher Himself, where is the special graciousness? What right had He to say "of such is the kingdom of heaven"? I maintain that any one of His hearers might, with quite as much right, have flatly denied it. But viewed as a Christian views it, the action is ineffably great because ineffably humble and loving, and redolent of that wholly indescribable depth and breadth of view of life and its issues, which characterized all that He said and did.

B. On my word! this is true: and how much hangs upon it! But let us look all round the question if we can. It is a commonplace among orthodox people that Christ revealed God. If so, it must have been by His actions and His words. Being divine they must have been perfect. Being a revelation of God, their perfection must be recognizable by man, something man can see to be perfection. Now are you not engaged in showing that the teaching was abortive and the actions, not trivial or indifferent but, humanly viewed, downright wrong? What, then, becomes of your revelation? How do you explain the origin of the belief that He was divine? His career on earth suddenly began to be public. The people did not know Him to be divine, but the effect of His actions and words was that they gradually thought Him to be so. But that could only have been because there was something transcendent in His personality and unimpeachably virtuous in His dealings with life's problems. On your showing, how could there have been any such result ? You see I am taking for the nonce the orthodox view and trying to show how it conflicts with your statements as to Christ's actions, humanly viewed, being imperfect or wrong. If people began by thinking Him divine, it would have been a different story. But they did not : and apologists are often concerned to show that they did not.

E. First let me correct one statement. The people in Palestine did not conclude Christ to be divine merely because His actions were good. Something very much more wonderful took place, which is connected, not with His outward example, but with the unspeakable fact of the giving of the Holy Spirit on the day of Pentecost. You remember that at the eve of Christ's ministry the number of believers were computed at "about 500": now on the day of Pentecost "3,000 were baptized"; and of these a large number could have known little or nothing of His actions and words. There is no hint of their being converted by any recital of His virtuous actions. If your statement were a complete statement of what took place, we should have found that the men and women, who were nearest to Him, formed the nucleus of believers, and that their number grew steadily during the three years. But the facts are otherwise. Nor could your picture give any explanation of the growth of the Church. It would follow from it that the further men were from the facts of His life, separated either by distance or time, the weaker became the impression of Him. But the contrary is the fact.

B. Well, but that upsets any explanation, surely.

E. No. If we bear in mind the saying that "there is a veil over all beginnings," and not expect so great a matter to be plain as a proposition of Euclid is plain, I think you will admit that the following statement is a truer way of putting the case.

As a matter of history, not of philosophy, or psychology, or modernism, or the like, we find that the "Good News" preached to the world by the Apostles in the dawn of Christianity, was a fact interpreted by a subsequent fact in a particular way. The first fact was that Jesus of Nazareth died on the Cross: the interpretation was that He did so to save men from their sins, and the subsequent fact which corroborated this interpretation was the Resurrection on the third day. Suppose we imagine things happening in that way: and then proceed to think how such an appeal, or rather statement, affected different people. As we are specially told, the interpretation became to the Jews a "cause of offence": perhaps because they thought it assumed too large a place for sin. The prevailing view was that the covenant nation needed no special cleansing, or, maybe, they could not reconcile the death with the idea of Christ's Messiahship. Probably those who accepted Christ as their Messiah became Christians, but many of them only did so because of the Resurrection, and the power of spiritual life which the early Christians showed. Their national pride prevented them from thinking much of the Death, anyhow in relation to themselves, as an Atonement. When we are further told that the Cross was "to the Greeks foolishness" we gather that the conventional feelings among the majority of Gentiles, or at the least Greek-speaking peoples, was equally antagonistic to the Gospel message. This may have been partly because it transcended reason, but the main objection must have been that they felt no particular need for what the

Apostles called the Remission of Sins. But along with these two large groups there were others. Can you not picture them?

B. I suppose you mean those who were inclined to bewail their sins? Surely not the best specimens of humanity?

E. They were those who were saved from underrating the fact of sin. They felt its profound mystery, its awful penetrative power, its close personal grip in the phenomena of remorse, guilt, and sense of individual responsibility; and, further, they felt its consequences, not only in widespread havoc and wreckage of life, in poisoning of relationships, in collapse of high endeavour, in dulling of hope, in defilement of innocence, in perplexities, silent anguish, drifting and despair; but in something more inward and searching than these, the prevailing sense of the loss of communion with God: a certain indescribable consciousness of crumbling ruin in the centre of man's spiritual being, touching not the understanding only—though there it transformed the thinking powers into empty bewilderment and contradictory negations—but the very dayspring of the highest region of man's being, his feeling of contact with the Source of all power, all growth, all joy. This deadly and disabling sickness was due to the tremendous fact that personal responsibility, bound up with freedom of the will, asserted itself against all palliations, subterfuges, doubt or denial, with an irresistible strength utterly and decisively victorious against man's reasoning and the assurances of his philosophical systems, empty, comfortless and unmeaning. Hence it was true for them as it undoubtedly is for us, that there is no problem in life worth mentioning, except the fact of sin, and when man looks forward to the strife which lies before him against ceaseless temptation and increasing weakness, or back on the woful record of failures, accounted for, but not in any way mitigated by, theories of heredity and a whole swarm of cheap fatalistic nostrums, there he finds himself faced by guilt in the past and the certainty of fresh collapse in the future.

B. Please go on. This is no mere historical statement, but true at the present day.

E. Imagine then an ordinary man possessed by such consciousness as this suddenly startled by the news of the Divine Son bearing this load of sin away, taking on to Himself all the guilt, the unspeakable horror and burden of the penalty of death inevitably attached to sin as its outcome and inevitable expression: when such a man heard that this amazing victory was wrought in the past as a finished triumph he would, of course, look upon life with new eyes of hope, and on this baffling world as a place redeemed by its Maker. But further, as he realized the challenge to himself that was involved in the story, that he should never again yield himself a victim to the fascination of sin or error, he would become aware of the cogent parsimoniousness of the message, in that it illustrated the three pregnant and uplifting words "God is Love" so powerfully that from thenceforth there was for him a motive of the most transforming potency in his life, the motive of free, willing service as the response of gratitude—simple gratitude for the proof of infinite love. Along with all this, which worked in him a completely new set of conceptions as to the why and wherefore of his own existence and the purpose of his being, there were also the grand assurances as to the truth of the revelation, in the manifestations of new life, cleansed hearts, braced up wills, and joyous confidence of self-surrender, shown by the members of the new community in which he was enrolled. Is it not fairly clear now that there were influences at work which would establish and quicken and inspire the faith within him till nothing could undermine it for all time?

B. And Humility?

E. I have not forgotten it. You see there are two ways in which the appearance of a new virtue might be accounted for. No Christian can refuse to believe in some kind of special interposition on the part of the Deity in human affairs at that time. One way of seeking an explanation, therefore, would be to assume a special activity of the Holy Spirit working on men's minds and souls, so that Humility appeared and was reverenced by all who came across it, just as a new form of courage and self-devotion appeared and was reverenced. Nor can any student of the narratives fail to notice that such must have been the case. But I cannot rest content with anything so mystical, unless we can point at the same time to the change in men's minds operating in a natural way. You see the difference?

B. You mean that you wish to arrive at something like a psychological explanation instead of resting on one simply supernatural.

E. Just so. I have little doubt that, in reality, the normal way in which the Divine Spirit works is in accordance with psychological laws; and that the supernatural is really in agreement with nature. But, leaving that on one side, let us consider the new view of life which must have dawned upon the converts from heathenism. In the first place you would agree, I think, that as long as salvation was presented to men as a thing to be won by their own efforts, so long there is room for what St. Paul calls "boasting," as the efforts appear to succeed?

B. Yes, but surely you don't mean that salvation is ever offered to man without effort on his part being required?

E. No, but the effort is not what is commonly supposed. Imagine a Jew, brought up by Rabbis to believe that in the Mosaic law, and its accretions through centuries, lay his guidance for life and hope of being finally saved. The first grand lesson he had to learn from the Apostles was that his salvation was already wrought—his sins already put away—his access to God freely opened. The marvel was already accomplished in the unseen world by One Who lifted the burden on to Himself in this world. On the part of the sinner all that was required was to "receive the reconciliation." Now if the matter went no further than this, is it not clear that he would be in the position of a child who realizes suddenly that through his father's love everything has been done for him?

B. Certainly: but is not that the exact description of a spoilt child?

E. Not at all. A spoilt child has everything done for him *without* realizing the element of love in the parents. He takes all the lavishness as a matter of course. But supposing he realizes that he deserves nothing of it, but that it is given as a free gift because his father loves all that is best in him, the effect would be to make him realize his own unworthiness.

B. I have long contended that the effect would be exactly the opposite. But I fancy I see that it must depend on the greatness of the gift, and the department of life to which it refers.

E. You are right. If the bounty were merely in the form of heedless pampering, no such effect would follow. But supposing it concerned the highest matters of which the child could conceive, and revealed at the same time not only the father's love but his wisdom, his justice, his power and forethought, what then?

B. Why, if the boy were of a good disposition and cared for these things he would, of course, feel himself unworthy of so much kindness.

E. There we have it. If the boy cares about such things; how much depends on that! But there is infinitely more in the Death of Christ than any illustration can possibly touch. The Apostles in their first lessons to the converts must have put the matter before them in this way: Think Who it was Who hung upon the tree in shame, helplessness and agony, all voluntarily undergone for you. He, the Divine One, bore your sins and the cost to Him was death; the death of the Son of God. You have first to realize the victorious love, and then take in the unutterable horror of sin which required such a ransom. That sin is the same sickening, depressing influence which bears down your life and poisons your soul, and which you deliberately encourage within you. It is supremely necessary for you to understand that the deliverance thus wrought was totally undeserved, in the sense that mankind had done nothing to earn it. All the heavenly life is now yours, if you care to have it: all your best hopes are fulfilled, if you will only believe what we say, because what we say was told us by the Eternal God Who cannot lie. Would not the effect on him be either that he would reject the whole message, or feel within himself an unworthiness such as he could not have conceived of before; and for two reasons. He would have to own his fellowship with the horrible thing sin, the malignity of which he was beginning to know: and further he would understand that nothing whatever in his life or conduct entitled him to claim the tiniest fragment of the gift which God so freely bestowed.

B. I think I see. You mean that if he rejected it, it would be because of his self-satisfaction: if he received it, it would mean a conviction of deep abasement and the very opposite of anything like self-congratulation?

E. Exactly.

B. I freely admit that your statement answers my original objection that the more God does for man the more the latter will be puffed up. But I have been so steeped in ideas as to man rising by his own efforts that your picture of a salvation, first accomplished by Christ and then merely received by man, is alien to all my ordinary thoughts. Somehow it strikes me as if true Christianity according to this should be an easy matter. Was Browning wrong when he called it hard?

E. He was undoubtedly right. But the hardness consists not, as people think, in dogged daily wrestling with temptation, or even with suffering, but in the changed view of life and its issues which alone makes it possible to face the temptations and the suffering. The Greeks gave the suggestive name of *μετανοία* to that change of view, and we have grievously impoverished the word by rendering it "repentance," which is only one department of *μετανοία*, though the most essential.

B. But why should the welcoming of this explanation of life be so difficult, when it speaks from beginning to end of a wonderful joy and hope, and of victory to which we *mortales aegri* are admitted?

E. It is difficult because it involves the uttermost self-abasements, the foregoing of every claim, the refusal to have recourse to any single form of human merit, as we call it (as if merit could be thought of as doing anything for us which Christ's work has left undone). It is true that when we look at the two things in fair perspective it is borne in upon us that there is something grotesquely presumptuous and insanely arrogant in man's first whittling down the supreme power of the Atoning Sacrifice offered by the Son of the Most High, and then inflating the importance of his puny strivings to better the world, or purify his own character, as if they were, in some sense, supplementing the deficiencies of Calvary. That is true: but the deceptiveness of the world's voices, its cajoleries, its flatterers and busy mockers combine together, with devilish skill and knowledge of the poor conceited human heart, to stir its pride; and among the agencies which are active in this bewildering warfare must be mentioned the presentment of Christianity, to the mass of people all over the world, under certain subtle perversions and disproportions, which allow of some mitigation of the self-abasement and self-conquest demanded by the New Testament teaching.

B. I am not sure that I follow you here.

E. (*after a pause*). If you attentively consider the temporary forms of popular Christianity, and all one-sided statements of the Gospel, I think you will find that they either flatter man's vanity directly by appealing to his natural instincts and congenital powers, or they tend indirectly to diminish the sense of dependence on God which is obviously the very foundation of humility.

B. As regards many of these—the modern ones at least—I have discussed them in regard to this very virtue, and found that they give no warrant for it whatever. But there is one variation, if I mistake not, on your presentment of the central teaching of Christianity, which is very commonly offered to the thoughtful public of to-day both in pulpits and numerous writings, and certainly there is a great deal of warrant for it in the New Testament. I am inexpert in theological phraseology, but I will try to explain.

The teaching I mean makes much less of the Death of Christ, but more of the spiritual renewal of mankind by a kind of union between the Risen Christ and the believer. Now clearly there is much said on this subject in the New Testament: and Christ's work so viewed is a theme which can only be sincerely published by a convinced Christian. Clearly it involves a belief in Christ's divinity. He is spoken of always as present with us now and helping men's infirmities by the infusion of a new life into his inner being.

Now why should not this renewal, this participation in the life of the True Vine be made conditional upon humility in the receiver? It seems reasonable to suppose that self-satisfaction in any shape would be a bar to the reception of grace: at least we are often told that Christ could only dispense His bounty on earth where there was a sense of need.

E. I am glad you have raised this question, since there is no doubt that a great deal of modern Christianity tends to exalt the work of the Ascended Christ at the expense of the Sacrifice offered in His Death, and this in a way not consonant with the teaching of the New Testament and the practice of the Apostles. It would take a very long time to discuss the proportion of space and emphasis allotted to the two subjects in Holy Writ, but we must restrict ourselves to noting that the place occupied by humility, self-abasement, etc., if the Ascended Life subject is taught in isolation from the Death of Christ, is very different from the place it occupies if the two are taught, as I am convinced they ought to be, in harmonious relation to each other. For, as you have clearly seen, the history of man's estimate of Humility requires some explanation of the sudden deepening of that estimate at the time of the introduction of Christianity. If it can be shown that one form of teaching would explain that phenomenon and the other would not, we have a solid argument in favour of the theory that the first form of teaching was delivered and believed by the earliest Christians.

B. Yes, that I suppose is so, and it adds a new interest to the subject.

E. Well, then, let us take the subject of the mystical union between Christ and the believer, and consider how much it makes of a claim for self-abasement on a convert to Christianity. Is it not fair to say that it is exposed to the difficulty you have seen from the first, viz. that man must think himself of great account if God thinks him worth renewing with His divine life through Christ? All exposition of the Love of God is exposed to this misunderstanding, except that which is based on the Atoning Death. For consider: in the one case man is told that he is daily being sanctified by the infusion of God's Life into his inner being. But plainly this might be true if there were no such thing as responsibility for sin, no haunting sense of guilt, in short, no Fall of Man, or whatever the *épouvantable mystère*, as Pascal, I think, called it, ought to be named.

B. You mean that according to the teaching of the mystical union only, no provision is made for the guiltiness of each man's past.

E. You see we must make clear under what aspect we regard sin. If you can persuade yourself that it is only a falling short of an ideal, simply an evidence that man is well-disposed but weak, then plainly there is no need to trouble your head about the meaning of the Atonement. But if you recognize that sin is wilful defiance of the highest thing the sinner knows, viz. law as the utterance of God's love and severity, that it is a choice of horrible evil by one who knows its horror, its deadliness, its stealthy poison, then it is impossible to acquiesce in the sufficiency of any theory which treats this heinous rebellion of God's children as if it had never been and merely explains how man's weakness is gradually turned into strength. Sin is either a hideous horror for which we are personally responsible, or it is merely imperfection. If it is the latter, then Christ died in vain: I mean that His was a superfluous death. The problem would have been adequately met if He had merely exhibited spotless virtue, taught with authority, promised men the rich bounty of the Holy Spirit, and ascended up into heaven. Where is the place for Humility in this scheme?

B. You claim, then, for the true Christian teaching, that, in respect of humility, it postulates first a certain doctrine as to sin which forbids self-congratulation, especially as the doctrine is corroborated by, if not based upon, general experience?

E. Yes. Amongst the reasons which have induced men to preach a less severe view of sin, I think we must assign a prominent place to the repugnance we naturally feel to any teaching which seems to impair our dignity. In full presence of facts which stagger and appal us with their damning evidence of man's insensate and foul depravity, we go on pluming ourselves on our dignified place in the Universe; so much so, that while the central message from God as to man's salvation is incontrovertibly bound up with a conviction of his helplessness and perversity, we are always struggling to retain what we think essential in the message and to whittle down the teaching of our helplessness, not because it is improbable, or unsupported by experience, but simply because it is derogatory to our fatuous self-importance.

B. I should think that could hardly be disputed. The bold irrationality of the general position is strikingly similar to that of many other currents of opinion among educated people.

E. Observe, then, that the teaching of the Atonement requires first a severe and humiliating belief as to the nature of sin. Secondly, that each man must recognize this taint, or disease of will, as his own.

B. Is that really so?

E. Beyond question it is so. The evil spirit who is continually tempting man to fend off from himself the true notion of sin, has recourse to a singular device, when the evidence from history or sociology brings that notion powerfully into our minds. It is this. It, or rather he, because I believe in a personal Enemy of mankind, draws as it were a kind of *vallum* round his central position, which, like the walls of Aurelian round Rome, is strong because it abandons all unnecessary outworks and encloses just the important minimum. Satan, in other words, allows the conviction of the heinousness and deformity of sin to lodge itself in a man's breast to the extent of recognizing those qualities of it plainly and with inerrancy in other people, but to leave the unhappy individual quite blind to the same phenomenon in himself. Just so you know people gifted with a sense of humour rich and delightfully alert, till it threatens to make fun of the *ego* : and then, with a grave but unhesitating firmness, the frivolous spirit is warned off the sacred area, as if its presence there would be something of a profanation. In the matter of the sense of sin, which is closely parallel to that of humour, the point is often reached where the malignity and deadliness of sin in other people is clearly and constantly discerned by eyes which seem quite blind when turned inwards. Now, of course, there is a general feeling that in such cases there is something very seriously wrong; but don't you think that we can now diagnose what is wrong with some certainty?

B. I am afraid I cannot go further than the popular verdict on such characters, which is that they are egoistic and decidedly unpleasant to have to do with. That is very generally felt.

E. Yes, or you might recall the solemn words about the Mote and the Beam in the Sermon on the Mount. But why did Christ speak so emphatically against the critical spirit in men? You may be sure that it was for some reason far deeper than that which you have given. Nor could we be satisfied with the explanation that the critical temper works harm in the relations of men with men. It is far from certain that it does: or rather it is quite arguable that its opposite, an easy contentment with other people's standard, is more mischievous. But even if it were clearly harmful, that would not be the answer to our question. Our Lord did not waste words on conduct that is clearly harmful, because such is generally condemned. Where He denounced, we find it was because the behaviour indicated a wrong relation towards God. So it was in this case.

B. Please explain.

E. Think of the words "Judge not that ye be not

judged." People, of course, are included[1]: they are not to be judged by Christians, lest the judges themselves be judged, not of course by men, but by God Himself. Now the matter which we can plainly see is the one concerning which God will judge the world, is the question as to the welcome, or the reverse, which men have given to the revelation of His love in the Sacrifice on Calvary. It is wholly inconceivable that an event of such transcendent magnitude—infinite Love revealed by infinite humiliation, and by the Prince of Life passing through the gate of death that we might live for ever—should be left to mankind to take into their hearts or to ignore just as they please. The work was done by the Saviour, but it cannot, as far as we can see, and as far as we have been told, operate for salvation in the case of those to whom it is an offence or simply a dull set of facts. In other words, the conceited and the hard-hearted are barred from its saving effect, because both alike are unconscious of their need. But no men are more unconscious of their need than those who can spend time, thought, and ingenuity in estimating the gravity of other men's shortcomings. Hence we can see that the propensity in this direction means *pro tanto* an incapacity to enter into the central,

[1] "People, of course, are included." This remark is based on a certain interpretation of the words in the Sermon on the Mount drawn from the context. Christ uses the words "Judge not" without any object; and we may connect them with the end of the preceding chapter, "Sufficient unto the day is the evil thereof" by supposing that having broadly mentioned evil and given a certain warning about it, He passes on to consider the Christian's attitude towards it. First negatively: whatever we may think of evil or do about it we are not to criticize the scheme of things which allows of it as if we had a right to say it might have been better; and, in the broad expression "evil," people are included.

simplest meaning of the Atonement. The critic of others cannot identify his own sin with the sin which Christ bore, otherwise he would be very, very tender towards sin in others, unless, of course, plain speaking to the face should be a necessity. But this is only a digression to show how intimately bound up the reception of the Atonement is with a deep self-abasement. I have mentioned two points in answer to our main question. There are clearly two more. The next would be that the teaching of the vicariousness of Christ's work is repellent to the natural man, not only because it is difficult to the intellect but because it leaves, comparatively, so little to our own efforts. "Without me ye can do nothing" is a saying which a proud man may tolerate, but certainly cannot understand.

B. But how would you answer this objection? You said just now that the work of Sanctification or the renewing of our lives by the Risen Christ is part of the Christian scheme? I mean, though you do not give it the first place, you admit that it is true and essential?

E. Certainly.

B. Why, then, do not the words you have quoted refer to this part of the scheme of Salvation as truly as to the Atonement wrought by the Saviour's Death? Preachers are always insisting that God's grace is everything, and man's efforts of no avail. Now surely that refers to the growth in goodness and not only to the initial stage when the Sacrifice for sin was offered; but I fear I am wording my thoughts very crudely.

E. Your meaning is quite plain. In more technical language we should say, Is not dependence on God quite as necessary for Sanctification as for Justification? Now a fairly complete answer for the purposes of our discussion would be that it might be, but that if so, it is much less manifestly so than in the matter of the Atonement, and consequently the theory would serve less well for an answer to our main question. You would probably admit that?

B. I think so, but of course one requires experience in these matters as in others. The warfare against pride certainly requires practice as much as any other warfare.

E. Indeed, that is most true. But we may surely go further and say that the process of Sanctification essentially demands at every step the full and complete co-operation of the individual. It is quite as much subjective as objective. You cannot conceive of God's grace operating through Christ on a man as if he had nothing to do with it. Every step in advance is *his* step; and if character is strengthened it is *his* character. There can be nothing fictitious about the growth in holiness, nor will it be long unperceived by others. It is quite possible for a struggling follower of his Master to be possessed by the idea of grace imparted by the Holy Spirit, an infinitely lavish bounty not given "by measure," but as soon as he is so possessed he runs a danger of pluming himself on the joyful though rudimentary evidences of a new vitality: then, immediately, the disease of introspection begins, or, if it does not, the equally fatal "boasting" of which St. Paul often speaks. Try to conceive of this teaching of grace being isolated from that of the Atonement, and I think you will see that the more it is emphasized *at the expense* of the latter the less likely it is to have added Humility to the catalogue of virtues.

B. Well, I suppose it would be open to the objection I formerly levelled against Christianity at large in this connexion, viz. that it presented a view of God taking infinite trouble for men without making any essential demand on them for self-abasement. Whereas if the Atonement is made the centre of the scheme there is such a demand.

E. That, I think, is quite a fair way of putting the difference.

B. Then if the doctrine of grace imparted through Christ is insufficient by itself to plant or foster the idea of humility, you would not, I suppose, refuse it a place in connexion with that of Atonement?

E. How could I possibly do so in view of the great space it occupies in New Testament teaching? Nay, I am strongly convinced that if taught in due relation to the other κατ' ἀναλογίαν τῆς πιστέως it ministers vitally and most effectively to this very end. The connexion between the two ought not to be difficult to seize. Suppose we take the phraseology of such a thinker as T. H. Green; it may help. He used to say that the process of Life through Death is an eternal divine process to be repeated by all the followers of Christ. Now what does Death here mean as applied to Christians? Certainly the death to sin, that is the starving or moyrtifing of that part of our being through which sin makes its assaults upon us and finds correspondence within us. I cannot restrict this part of us to the body, though doubtless there is a close connexion between the body and sins of sensuality. But when we think of the other great department, sins of pride, then I think the process would be correctly described as a death to Self: the very essence of which is exactly what we mean by Humility, or the denying of Self. The expression covers not only the controlling of fleshly desires of all sorts, but the ignoring of the spiritual self in its claims for recognition, for personal prominence, praise of men and so forth.

B. Yes, but what is the exact bearing on our question?

E. Why, this. If you take the doctrines of the Mystical Union, and the Inclusive Humanity of Christ, to use Moberly's expression, and the gradual attainment of self-mastery which we see in Christian lives, it might be possible, as we have said, to make out a case against them, that they are not directly antagonistic to self-congratulation and boasting. But, in reality, that all falls to the ground as soon as we discern the underlying relation between them and the Atonement. "The Eternal process of Life through Death" would not be understood at all by men, had not our Lord manifested it in a special way, that is, in relation to the universal phenomena of sin. Not, I mean, that the Death is to be regarded as merely a stage which has to be traversed on the way to life, any more than Sin is merely a stage on the way to perfection: but the Death of Christ was infinitely more: it was an Atoning Death for all mankind, as well as a gate of entrance into everlasting life, or rather it was the latter because it was the former. Similarly the death to self of the true followers of Christ is a death which is not only a passage to life, but has an atoning power as well. This has often been remarked. But the relevant thing to notice now is that the mystical union with the Risen Lord means a union with One Who is the eternal exemplar of the divine process spoken of: so that, in so far as we have grasped the fact of the Atonement, we can feel certain that union with Christ means, subjectively, death to self. This is the certain and inevitable issue of setting the two great mysteries in true relation to each other.

B. But ought there not to be some distinct reference to this view of the facts somewhere in the New Testament?

E. Undoubtedly, if you were to read closely you would find many. Perhaps this one will now suffice. The first eight chapters of the Epistle to the Romans consist of a profound exposition of the two mysteries, man being justified by faith in the Atoning Death, and made holy by union with the ascended Life of Christ. Then follow three chapters of discussion of the position of the Jewish nation, and in the twelfth the Apostle proceeds to point out what bearing the doctrine must have on the moral lives of his readers. It is striking to observe the prominence given to Humility. First, the inclusive precept "that ye present your bodies a living sacrifice," then "that ye be transformed by the renewing of your mind," which seems to mean the *μετανοία* we spoke of just now; and then observe the words "for I say through the grace given unto me to every man that is among you not to think of himself more highly than he ought to think." This is among the very first precepts based on the exposition of the effects of the Atoning Death, and the operation of the Risen Life. In the words which follow, the connexion is brought out; "but to think so as to be sober minded; to each as God distributed a measure of faith." The words are not easy to understand fully, but there is little doubt that the reception by the individual of a gift of faith is made the basis of an appeal to him not to be proud.

B. Would you kindly let me look at the passage? I do not see how you can be sure that the Apostle is not basing his appeal on the renewal of life in the Christian community; in other words on what he conceived to be the work not of the Atoning but of the Risen Christ.

E. My point is that you must not sharply distinguish the two as far as our present question is concerned. What can we suppose he means by " faith " here? Faith in what? Why in Christ our Saviour; and Saviour means one who saves from sin, and that expression must be to some extent retrospective. In other words a sinful man must have a conviction that the way of access to God *has been* opened for him—that is the Atonement—before he can rely on the promise of imparted grace, that is the work of the Ascended Christ. But if we are to be guided by the New Testament we must attribute this conviction in the mind of proud, sinful men to the influence of the Holy Spirit; so that the work of the Spirit is primarily the enabling man to apprehend what Christ did. The apprehension is an interpretation of man's spirit by the Holy Spirit.

B. Is not that going further than is legitimate?

E. What else can be the meaning of the great words " He shall take of Mine (or " of Me ") and shall show unto you." " He shall glorify Me: for He shall receive of Mine and shall show unto you." " The Spirit of truth which proceedeth from the Father, He shall testify of Me." We have agreed that the work of Christ which the Holy Spirit was to perpetuate, was not merely teaching, nor setting a sinless example, but a redemptive work, and the showing of that work to mankind means the bringing it home to man's innermost heart. Or, to borrow the language adopted by those supposed to be of a different school, suppose we conceive of the renewal of mankind by the Holy Spirit as the imparting of the life of Christ, it yet remains true that the life was that of One who had passed through death. So with this thought in view, equally whether it is the apprehension of the Atonement, or the reception of the new life, the Christian finds that thoughts of self, about self, and for self, dwindle away in the process called by St. Paul " the renewing of the mind." The mind is indeed renewed: it is absorbed in adoring contemplation of——

B. Pardon my interrupting; but it is a phrase like that which is so desperately puzzling to a modern Englishman who may be thoroughly well disposed to Christianity, and may even have some knowledge of the inadequacy that there is in the popular notions of it. No matter how rich is your presentation of the faith, can you possibly avoid exaggeration if you speak of Christians with their minds *absorbed* in contemplating heavenly mysteries. Think of all the scores of people you must have met with, splendid characters and the very backbone of the nation in zeal, intelligence and self-devotion to high causes; they are admirable and whole-hearted citizens, but where is the absorption? They are immersed in things that are excellent, but almost wholly of earth.

E. Remember that though I use the present tense we are really in quest of the force which brought Humility into the category of the highest virtues. Doubtless such a phrase as I have used is true nowadays only of a very few; but don't they lead the rest just as they did in St. Paul's day? At any rate keeping to our subject let us see if the following is not a fair statement of what did and does still occur in the case of choice souls. They become, some suddenly, some gradually, possessed by the facts of the bounty of God's salvation prepared for mankind and being even now worked out in history. They, more and more, set their affections on a process which not only clears the heaven for them in respect of their individual needs, but gives manifold hints of things inexpressible, of an economy which the highest thoughts of man cannot compass or describe. While they worship and adore, the mortifying of the corrupt affections is going on: it is an inevitable concomitant of true worship that the spell exercised upon them by the "old man" fades and dwindles as they turn on it eyes strengthened to gaze at the true light which streams from a higher region, not the flickering glare of the earthly vision.

B. And by the "old man" you mean virtually the love of self?

E. Exactly; though it shows itself, of course, in many different and subtly disguised shapes. But there you have the blending of the two subjects of the Atonement for sin, and the progressive sanctification of the Christian. The temper taught by the story of the Atonement is that of "wonder, love and praise," and experience shows that in that temper Sanctification progresses, but as soon as man contemplates his own progress as if he could claim credit for it, so soon it is checked and perverted. Now he must recur to the objectivity of the Atonement that his mind may be again renewed and the daily work of the Holy Spirit within him be understood. *Sic itur ad astra!*

B. Sir, I thank you with all my heart. You have given me ideas too rich and wonderful for my poor brain to seize, but by the help of the Spirit of wisdom I trust they will become lights to guide me from earth to heaven. Good-bye.

E. Good-bye; in the oldest meaning of the words.

B walked home and no sooner had an hour to himself than he put the question plainly into words: Have

I been cajoled by the gentle voice and wisdom of a very attractive old man, or has he given me the solution of a great problem? Here is a quality the learning of which, and even the recognition of which, seems clean contrary to such general instincts of mankind as prompt them to self-assertion, self-esteem, self-defensiveness, self-consciousness. For many centuries the recognition of the quality among the foremost pagans was in abeyance. But immediately after the events on which Christianity is founded, it is deeply planted in men's minds and the quality itself though perpetually derided, thwarted, scorned and misunderstood, has never been extinct, and it is now obviously taken to be the very centre of the Christian character and the purest outcome of its influence. If I am asked for an explanation of this change, I cannot merely acquiesce, in a vague form of words, that it is due to the influence of Christianity, though it undoubtedly is; but I must seek some more cogent, more penetrating answer. That I find to be here. Granting a rudimentary instinct in its favour, the excitation of that instinct was brought about by men's being enabled to apprehend the revelation of God's Love. Conceit among children, boys and young men is sometimes indomitable, but when it is really overcome, it is not by proofs of inferiority or by defects in competition, but by being brought to realize that some one whom they deeply respect is full of an immense unshakable love for them, of the kind which is incessantly exacting in its demands, but deeply considerate, and helpful, though grave and even severe. If such an influence can inspire unselfishness in young hearts, it is because they are ashamed to be selfish any longer. Something in the contact with real self-forgetfulness wakes up the feeling for others which is the parent of humility in the natural man. But, of course, this is only an utterly pale and feeble reflection of the appeal of the Cross. So, speaking from the side of man, we may say that the Cross saves by inspiring us with the conviction of God's Love. But that conviction rests on a deeper one: viz. that somehow that Death was the unlocking of the door between us and God which sin had barred and bolted. We may not understand more than a very little of *how* this can be; but certain it is that everything depends on believing it; and for the believing it, humility is required, as it is believed humility grows and grows. Moreover I learn, what I never imagined before, that there is the closest possible relation between this Atoning Death and the work of the Risen Christ. As His teaching was bound to be quite useless but for the influence of the Holy Spirit, so the purpose of His Death would be thwarted by sheer indifference on our part, except for the same influence and transcendent power. Again; while belief in this power grows, humility must become more and more a fact to the believer; for he finds by plain experience that as his pride dies away in a joyous and confident self-surrender, in like measure a new life is given him and he recognizes the gift of the Eternal Joy promised by his Lord.

The present age is intently occupied with the study of itself. Much that is useful is the outcome, but it is clear that the sickliness of self-consciousness is a real present-day disease, the morbid issue of this widespread temper. We are craving for something deeply recreative and invigorating, and yet here to our hand is the inexhaustible truth of the eternal gospel: the objective truth which yet must become our own; the truth imparted to a community and yet the personal property of each individual, which, for its first timid welcoming as well as for its full reception, alike demands, and at the same time bestows, the Divine power of self-forgetfulness.

The need is great and all pervading, and so is the sense of that need. The real marvel, the only puzzle which admits of no solution is that man, who apparently is so conscious of his disease, is so wofully unready to admit that the remedy is a remedy; that while he shudders at the abyss of despair, he is always inclined to war against his one hope. One would expect him to give any message of hope a favourable hearing, considering that hope, joy, confidence and the like, are the very things for which he yearns. Yet lo! the mass of mankind are engaged not in fighting as they once did to spread what they believed to be true, but in whittling down what they individually profess, till it is emptied of all elements of hope and retains only its qualities of severity and urgent demand.

So it has always been. When the first tidings of the Saviour were brought by the Wise Men to Jerusalem, we read that the king was moved and all Jerusalem with him, but not to welcome, only to murder or blank indifference. St. Paul too said with perfect truth, "For the hope of Israel I am bound with this chain"; not for Israel's disappointment, but for their hope. Strange that mankind, like Wordsworth's child, is "thus blindly with his blessedness at strife"! Is it not true that of all the perplexities of life this is the only one really stubborn and permanent? The ever baffling fact not that man does wrong, but that he obstinately sets himself to *think* wrong? The doing follows from the thinking and is no mystery whatever; but the thinking wrong, in these lofty matters which we have been considering, is indeed a sore and weary puzzle. The only clue to the mystery is in the plain fact that we naturally dislike any truth which warns us that we are not self-sufficient; and just when the Christian creed becomes charged with eternal hope for poor wayward humanity, it reminds us that, vast though our responsibility is, the victory over evil has been won by Another.

Thus it was that B thought he had received his answer to the question, but the life which was now his to live, as time went on, taught him new elements of truth. It was not only that in his everyday individual warfare against egoism, to which he was moved by the constraining love of Christ, he grew in the sense of Humility as an essential outcome of Christianity, learning that without it he could learn nothing vitally and fruitfully of the Atonement or of the exultant working on the human heart to which has been given the name of the mystical union with Christ. More than this, he for the first time realized that he was an incorporated member of a Society on earth which the same Divine Lord had wonderfully endowed with His own life, breathing into it the very breath of God's own Spirit: a Society working and travailing here below in spreading the news of the Redemption of man from sin and marching forward like a great army in all the glad assurance of a triumph already won, with its battalions mysteriously linked with the unnumbered hosts of faithful men and women who have passed beyond the veil. He found that this Society demanded from each and all of its members the humbleness of co-operation and corporate activity, in a spirit not unlike that which inspires a great orchestra interpreting some imperishable utterance of a master-mind under the spell of a powerful and sympathetic conductor: in such manner that any self-assertion on the part of the least or the most skilled among the players is a marring of the entire effect and a disloyalty to the law under which alone they can hope to bring the thoughts of genius into the hearts of their fellow-men. In thus living more and more in the warmth of this unity with other Christians, B found that the difficulties which had hitherto barred him from understanding the claim of the Church upon his goodwill and ready service were fundamentally the same old hindrances as in other matters, springing from self-love, dislike of sinking self, preference for criticising others rather than for fellowship in labour, in thought, in self-denial.

It was these hindrances that made it hard for him fully to take in, not only that the world was a redeemed place, but that it was redeemed through, and in, an Ecclesia. Egoism still prompted him to deny first the fact of Redemption—though by now he had outgrown that delusion—and then the method on which the gathering of the fruits of Redemption by mankind depended. It seemed easier to substitute some other method than that of the Society, and yet his intellect told him there was no warrant for doing so. In B's case the mind was persuaded first, and then the heart turned.

Again, B found that in one great department of Church life the challenge to the egoist became yet more urgent and searching than ever. In the Eucharist he found himself face to face with an Institution derived straight from the Lord and Master of Christians, demanding of him first a submission of intellect, then a surrender of life. It was not difficult for him to accept the Lord's

Supper as a purely commemorative feast, and to attend it when convenient, vaguely as part of the Church life in which he was beginning to find joy. But to learn the inner truth that the outcome of the Atonement, the participation and growth in the Life of the Risen Christ, was, by Christ's special ordinance, bound up with this particular Institution was a fresh demand on his sacrifice of himself. It called on him to recognize his helplessness in a definite form, concrete though spiritual, and right on through the coming years it was never anything but an affront to his pride to admit this truth, though he had long before made his intellect bow to it and confess its dominance. Now he felt its power too. The more he drank in the wondrous teaching, handed down by a long line of witnesses and ambassadors in the name of Christ, the more vitally he perceived that the Institution was an embodiment of the great words "He that loseth his life shall find it."

Such, in brief outline, was the story of B's conversion. He was brought to a sense of profound tranquillity and inward peace by learning the correspondence between his own fundamental needs and the good tidings committed to the Christian community. So the egoist became not merely an altruist but a δοῦλος δούλων Χρίστου, gratefully and joyfully taking the lowest place; and as his affections were more and more set on the manifestation of the Love of God, his self-regard, with all its delusions and chicanery and disappointments, died away. The change of this great renewal was deep and complete; but outwardly there was not, for a time at least, anything very startling for his friends to notice. He went on doing useful things and being pleasant to others, *non aliter*

quam si clientum longa negotia
dijudicata lite relinqueret,
tendens Venefranos in agros
aut Lacedæmonium Tarentum.

But in his heart he knew that for him the life eternal was begun.

CHAPTER VII

A Year After

DURING the year that followed B's momentous conversations with E, he read extensively and devoted his mind to the question how to bring the principles he had learnt into close contact with his daily life, and especially with the bringing up of his children. Briefly, it may be said that instead of the problems dwindling in number and complexity they seemed to increase in both respects. His children developed unexpected tempers and a waywardness that often bewildered him, and at present he could not say that he found himself more sympathetic with the very humdrum people who dropped in upon him from time to time for some talk. But in regard to the last, he noted that he could abstain far more readily than before from the trick of slightly scornful description, which no longer amused him as it used to do, when indulged in by others. And at home, though his conception of evil was immensely deepened, and there was growing up in him something that may be called a horror of sin, yet he inclined more and more to large and tolerant feelings when things went awry; not in the least that he became lax: quite the reverse; but the thought of a child's relation to God, which was now habitually present with him, reminded him ever of the *patience* of the Almighty Father, the gradualness of His method, and the eternity which lies before a human soul. So that while

B's life was outwardly but little altered, a few friends perceived some deep change; but no one was able to say what it was, nor did any one of them try to do so.

One day an old friend of B's, who had been travelling in the Dominions with the intention of collecting evidence as to the possibility of Imperial Federation, wrote to propose himself for a visit, and being heartily welcomed stayed with B for a week, and greatly they enjoyed themselves talking over the future of the British Empire, as well as numerous questions of a more domestic kind. The visitor, whom we will call F, soon noted the change in B, and determined to try to probe a little way further into his mind than he had yet ventured to do, especially as, on his own subjects, he was conscious of an indefinable languor in the interest B displayed. While to himself the attitude of Canada towards the problem of an Imperial fleet was absorbingly and pressingly urgent, B seemed, with all his knowledge and well-balanced judgment, to be inclined towards an indefinitely waiting policy: as if the conduct of affairs in this and other questions were not a matter for which he and F were directly responsible.

So F began, in the middle of a long and lovely walk among the uplands of Buckinghamshire near Beaconsfield, to question his friend on this kind of detachment from affairs of real moment. How is it, said he, that you and I, though we agree on so many abstract questions, and are not ranged on opposite sides in politics, yet could never manage to become fellow-workers in a great practical cause?

B. I could work, I think, with any one, certainly with you, in any practical cause to which I felt sure I was called.

F. Called? You mean in the sense in which a young man feels himself called to the ministry of the Gospel?

B. Exactly. You are busied in matters which very likely are of importance to the country, but I am convinced that my energies are required elsewhere; or rather I should not say required, but that God tells me to devote them elsewhere, and that of course settles the question for me. Moreover, I am by no means so confident as I once was, that the efforts men have made and are making for the amelioration of society, are really of importance; I don't at all mean that they ought not to make them, but it often surprises me to see how different are the issues of any human endeavour from what was anticipated.

F. But what has brought you to this tone of feeling? At some other time I should like to follow out your suggestion, but do tell me first how it is you look at things now from some point of view which I find it difficult to designate; perhaps I should say it is less human than it used to be.

B. Putting it very briefly, I have been through an experience, some of which is quite indescribable, but the rest, being more of an intellectual matter, can be explained. Something led me to investigate the ethical foundation of a very central virtue, to which we give the name Humility, and I found after much thought and discussion that it was based on a vital feeling for the message of Christianity, viz. that the Divine Maker and Governor of the world has revealed Himself as a God of Love.

F. Do you mean that the elementary virtue, as I should call it, of not being conceited, really depends for its continuance on a strong conviction, that that message is true, not only in a historical sense, but as a present life-giving influence ?

B. Certainly ; but it would take some time to give the reasons at all fully.

F. I should be interested to hear them. But I think I ought to tell you first of my own position in these matters, which, like yours, has been affected by experience, but in a very different way. You see, one has been coming across a mixed lot of people in the Colonies and all over the place, and among them I have found some excellent specimens ; vigorous, keen citizens of the Empire. But it must be admitted that in the matter of religion, as far as I can make out, and in the sense in which you would use the word, they are wanting. They would describe your present views and feelings as mystic or dogmatic, and would shrug their shoulders, not in contempt at all, but from a sense that they move in a different world. There are thousands of the best Englishmen who would do the same, and I am bound to say when I hear you utter such sentiments, that I am perfectly aware they refer to emotions which I have never known, and which I really believe I was not made to know.

B looked at his friend's bronzed honest face, and fine vigorous frame, and thought of his life devoted to the noble aim of strengthening his country's position in the world. It was plain to him that he had before him one of those grand Englishmen who, absorbed in what is to them the highest thing they can understand, are inevitably, as it seems, bound to leave the doctrinal part of religion out of their range of vision. He knew by this time that any attempt to widen such a horizon was likely to end either in failure or in a certain weakening of the simple strong personality. But, finding F was not unwilling to pursue the subject, he thought it best to let him utter his misgivings, anticipating that he would utter something which was not foreign to his own experience. So he asked him, Do you mean that these sentiments lie outside of your mental vision, or that you have reason to doubt their truth?

F. Not the latter. I am willing to grant that there must be some deep truth in them, because I have seen more than once the astonishing effect for good their acceptance has had on people. Not, of course, that this is anything of a scientific proof. But I am not one of those who require a scientific proof for Christian doctrine. There is nothing in those doctrines which I find difficult of belief, if I restrict the word to the intellect. The evidence for them is very strong, and, in short, when I see a great many hard-headed logical people clinging to them still, after 1,900 years, as vigorously as ever, it is enough for me. But where I come short is in the personal grasp of them: the mind within me is not built on these lines; it seems to me that whereas some men and a great many women naturally take these notions in, as part of their deepest instincts, or at least of these feelings, others are constructed so as to hold them in a kind of second-hand fashion, not because they really understand them or have experience of them, but because they know what they have done to make other men's lives admirable. Further than this we cannot go, and speaking for myself I am pretty sure that I was not intended to go further. So I give myself up to hard work, hoping to be of some use in my generation.

B. Do I understand that you would then take up a position antagonistic to what I was saying about Humility? You remember the exact argument: that the set of qualities, called by that name, were plainly observable, only after the great facts on which our religion is based were taken deep into men's hearts, and that anything short of this, such as a mere intellectual acquiescence in the doctrinal statement, or the vague Deism that existed before Christ, was quite powerless to produce anything at all like them. But as they are now universally felt to be essential to the highest virtue, there is a very strong ground for supposing Christian doctrine to be, not only true, but something we are bound to take deeply into our hearts, if we possibly can.

F. No, I am not antagonistic to that statement. It seems to me a solid and important argument for the truth of those doctrines, that the vital recognition of them produced so undeniably fair a fruit. But it is quite compatible with that acknowledgment, to hold that the power so to receive the doctrines is only given to a minority, while the recognition of the virtues, which the doctrines, so received, bring into evidence, and further the practising of those virtues, are in the power of all.

B. That is to say, you would favour the view that the teaching of Christ was virtually esoteric: intended for the few who could understand?

F. That has always seemed to me the meaning of "He that hath ears to hear let him hear"; and again, "To you it is given to know the mysteries of the kingdom of Heaven: but to those that are without in parables."

B. Nay, if you think further you will see that neither text bears that meaning. "He that hath ears," etc., is an injunction to all who are listening to do their best to understand. Christ recognized that there were many who did not understand, but He never acquiesced in the fact as if it were a part of a contemplated scheme. Similarly "to those that are without": it was a necessity, as He soon found, to speak to the multitudes in parables; but you get no evidence that He was ever anything but distressed at the fact. Finally, what meaning could we, under this hypothesis, attach to the command "Go ye and teach all nations"? It is, of course, an old controversy. I think I am right in saying that whenever in Christendom the esoteric theory has been consistently acted on, the results have been disastrous.

F. But, surely, you cannot mean that it is incumbent on all Christians alike to study dogma?

B. The words express something quite foreign to my meaning. Suppose we put it in this way. There is no truth so difficult to grasp nor so transforming to human life when it is grasped, as that contained in the words God is Love. Now the revelation of God the Father given by Christ is a revelation of that very truth. If that is admitted, and I do not gather that you at any rate deny it, how can there be any limit to the claim upon each one of us to make the truth his own? Consider this. If God is Love, then it would contradict His nature that He should *as part of His divine scheme* restrict the knowledge of His Love to a minority of the human race. Yet that is what the esoteric theory means. I grant freely and fully that appearances favour the belief that scores of our countrymen are not intended to have any perception, by experience, of mysticism. But that is only part of the puzzle of the world. It is a very different thing to recognize a vast defect, and to assume it is part of God's scheme for the world. Moreover, the view of the relation between God and man which I am advocating, is inherent in the very essential meaning of the word Love.

F. I do not follow you.

B. I mean that the very nature of Love is to demand a response from the object of the love. To use the word with any other implication would be a gross misuse of language; to use it of God, as Christ did, unless He meant that God requires His Love to be answered by ours, would be to deceive men in the very greatest subject of all: to raise the greatest imaginable hopes and then to dash them by showing that the wonderful word meant something quite different when used of God from what it means among men.

F. Well, I admit there is sound logic in that. But suppose one can't return the love?

B. Go back to the figure of the father and the child. Can you imagine a really loving father content that his child should go on growing up without the faintest effort or wish to return the feeling which he shows to him continually? What is the normal process? Is it not that the child is made to notice his father's tenderness and care for him, and the response is looked for sooner or later as a matter of course. Now the adult Christian is called upon to read, mark, learn, and inwardly digest the evidences of his Heavenly Father's love for him, in the Bible, in Nature, in his own spiritual experience, and the history of the Society to which he belongs. All that is the study of God's revelation of Himself; but it is not to end there. It is without meaning or purpose, unless it is to lead to a vital response of love being made to Love. Further—and this is a fair plea to use to any one who recognizes the truth of Christ's teaching—if, in the case of a child and a human father, the excuse would not be admitted for a moment that the child *could* not return the love, what right have we to suppose that God can tolerate in us the frigid acquiescence, of which you speak, in a relation which we have never taken the first steps thoroughly to understand?

F (*after a pause*). You certainly put forcibly the case for giving attention to the matter. But I doubt if any one who has, as you have, something of the receptivity for mysticism, can possibly understand the blank impotence that another may be conscious of, in regard to any emotional response to an approach made to him by the Invisible God.

B. Pardon me; I do not lay stress on the necessity of the emotions being warm and responsive, but rather on the recognition of the plain duty, the very highest that we possibly can recognize, of putting forth the utmost effort of mind and will to understand the evidence of God's Love. The choice spirits, you admit, understand it by experience. Very well; then those who have not that experience are bound to make up for it as far as they possibly can, by exercising not their emotions, but their minds; instead of which you make your emotional disability an excuse for leaving the other faculty in abeyance. Conceive, my dear friend, the terrible weakness of your intellectual position, in granting so much, but refusing to see what it involves. Is it really the fact that you accept the teaching of our Lord as to God's Love; you do not deny at all the divinity of the Saviour Himself; in other words, you admit the facts on which our knowledge of God's Love is mainly based, and then can find it in yourself to give *all* your thoughts, hopes, energies and the like to a wholly different set of subjects and activities, leaving the most glorious truth that has ever illuminated the soul of humanity not acknowledged and disbelieved, but acknowledged and forgotten? How can that be anything but disloyalty to your understanding?

F. Well, but you see the difficulty. The kind of personal contact with an invisible Being which is evidently granted to some people, is denied to me and to scores and thousands of others. What can we do but accept the raised ethical standard which the illuminated consciousness of the favoured few has given us, and set our lives to conform to it?

B. You are still confusing the service of emotion and the service of mind. We agree that, speaking roughly, some are unequipped by nature for the former; some, on the other hand, are able for both kinds; but is there any educated man who is unprovided with faculties for the latter? The slightest realization in his own mind of the majesty, the penetrating and almost irresistible power of the truths in the Apostles' Creed, must convince you that however cold and prosaic and practical you may fancy your temperament to be, here is a claim on your very highest energies which may not be set aside; I don't mean the sinking of yourself into the rapture of an Oriental mystic, or even of one of the lights of our own firmament, Catharine of Siena, St. Francis, or Julian of Norwich; but the claim is upon you as a man able to think, to grow daily in the practice of letting your sense of duty be transformed by the influx of the light from heaven. This can be done and often is done by the typical Northern English Christian who brings to the consideration of the subject some balance of faculties peculiarly his own. He combines a warmth of heart with a strong reserve and a very distinct loyalty to duty. *Ex hypothesi*, he is so far an educated man that he can set two and two together, reason and infer. Moreover, you must, if you adhere to your position, be false to your own faith. How can you call yourself a believer in Christ's teaching, unless you see that He kept exactly this kind of character-problem in view, when He said "Ask and ye shall receive, seek and ye shall find: knock and it shall be opened unto you," or "If ye then being evil know how to give good gifts unto your children; how much more shall your heavenly Father give the Holy Spirit to them that ask Him?" Think, too, of the bearing of all His teaching on the importunity of a real Christian's prayer.

F stopped in his walk and looked for a time over a gate at a lovely landscape where the ground sloped gradually through copse, meadow and byre towards the great river valley. Beyond the silver waters, stretched the blue woods, and further still the uplands of the southern country crowned with beech and fir groves. You mean, said he, something considerable in the way of study and thought, besides prayer. That is a programme which I readily admit that I have not put into practice. But before speaking of the adequacy of the more ordinary practical kind of life, let me ask you for more warrant from the teaching of Christ for the pressing of this claim; unless you think that as to our own innate perceptions there is more to be said.

B. Certainly there is. Can't we put the two sets of grand facts side by side; first the avowed compulsion of the moral law, and our own weakness of will in presence of it, and the manifold failures of life which are definitely due to that very weakness. Secondly, the amazing glory of the Creator's manifestation of His own Love, and, in us, the transfiguring of painful and uncertain service to law into the spontaneous growing knowledge of an Infinite Person. If He Who made us, has put the knowledge of these sublime facts within our reach, how can there be any further debate as to the main duty of a believing man? What can our acknowledgment of God amount to, if it stops short of recognizing that when once He has revealed His nature to His own creatures, and given them faculties of thought and prayer, no duty can take precedence of that which bids us "lay hold of eternal life"? Having received some measure of the "unspeakable gift" do we not feel that we are in the world that we may pass it on to others? Now that is an inference strictly in congruity with our own reason.

F. Yes, I will admit it to be so. But still you may be begging the question without meaning to do so. How do you know that for many of us the best way to know God personally is not to devote our lives to dutiful service of an impersonal kind? It looks to me as if that is the utmost that can be expected of us in this world; that is to say, till such time as He allows the thick veil to be withdrawn, presumably by death.

B. There are two answers to be given to that question. The first would be drawn from the practice of those who have genuinely belonged to the divine Society called the Church, and from the guidance which their teaching and example give. The second from further teaching in the New Testament, where, as I have said, the particular problem before us has been dealt with, and woe betide us if we set aside the warning!

F. I should like to hear those points developed. Bear in mind, what I should imagine is incontestable, that there has been during the last fifty years a vast increase of interest in ethical questions and a dwindling of interest in theology; at least, if one may judge from popular periodicals and the prevalent style of preaching.

B. Your remark, I fancy, is anything but incontestable; but let it pass for the present. Assuming it to be true, it only means that there is an urgent demand on all of us to resist a powerful current of erroneous opinion. At least that is the light in which I feel bound to interpret the situation. To my mind, history shows with extraordinary vividness that any great social advance made by mankind has been the outcome of a deeper grasp on those religious notions which are often stigmatized as mere dogma. Most people would allow this to be true in respect of such virtues as purity of life, respect for womanhood, abhorrence of slavery, and so forth. What I have recently learnt is that the beautiful and fundamental qualities of Humility are even more certainly to be traced to that teaching of Christianity which is not merely ethical, not even ethical in the richest and loftiest sense of the word, but is simply religious; concerning as it does primarily, not the relation of man with man, but of man with God. Well, allowing your diagnosis to pass that people are far more interested in ethics than in religion, I am bound to infer from my experience of human history that they are interested in the building but not in the foundation; in the leaves, while they forget the root of the tree and the soil.

F. Yes, but is this the first of your two points? Did you not say you referred to the unanimous practice of genuine members of the Church?

B. Yes. My digression into the other matter was only to justify my remark that, if you are right in your estimate of the favourite subject at the present day, it is, to me, a serious duty to rectify the popular judgment as far as I can.

F. I quite see. Now for the other point.

B. It is very simple. Do we not invariably find that the practice of the Church has been to plant certain truths and let them work their effect in social life? I don't mean that, always and everywhere, Churchmen have been wise enough to follow out this second part literally, but where the Church has been at its best those have been the main principles of its work on earth. Look at the indisputably strong corroboration of what I say which is afforded us by the work of Christ; and afterwards by that of St. Paul.

F. You mean that whereas the triumphant effect of Christianity was not only in the elevation of human character, but in the purifying of social customs, yet we must recognize that Christ abstained wholly, and St. Paul to a considerable degree, from preaching social reform.

B. Exactly; and about St. Paul, it is certain that whenever he gave instructions as to moral conduct he adopted a very peculiar position which we should nowadays be inclined to distrust as being over-dogmatic. It was this. He never addressed his converts on moral problems without treating them as members of a Society which had been divinely illuminated. And further you know, of course, that the moral portion of his Epistles comes at the end of each if it comes at all, after a full exposition of some aspect of divine Grace, and often introduced by the word "therefore."

F. I think I heard that when I was at the University, but I had forgotten it.

B. You see also that the inference from it is that our duty is to plant the truth, not to stimulate by exhortation the flagging morality of the age, which flags because it lacks root. To plant the truth, I say, and let the effect of it be what it may upon the numberless complexities of modern life.

F. Yes, I think that would perhaps be a fair inference.

But are you right in saying that such has always been the action of the Church with regard to theology and moral improvement ?[1]

B. I don't say theology; but the handing on of the main message of our Lord, viz. that God is Love, and that He Himself, though divine, lived a human life quite consistently inspired throughout by that religious belief. His Life and Death and Resurrection have made it possible for us to do the same.

F. That is, of course, just the point where I fail to follow. You lapse into mysticism there, and I am fain to fall back on my conviction that for many of us such talk is meaningless, and that the best thing we can do is to confine ourselves to social work and the like, while freely acknowledging that others do get life and strength from these dogmas which escape us. I should go further and say that we ethical people are really living upon a moral quickening which has in the past been due to the religious teaching of definite dogmatic Christians. But may we go back to the Church's practice ?

B. There is much that I could say, but it would take us into some controversial regions, and after all the example of Christ in such a matter must be supreme. How otherwise than on this principle do you explain His refusal to interfere in the dispute about property which was brought directly to Him ?

F. Well, I suppose He had set the teaching of religious truth before Him as His main task, and any dispute of

[1] Twenty-five years ago I heard Archbishop Benson say that St. Gregory of Nazianzus, when asked to what he attributed the great moral improvement of the town in which he lived, said, "To the consistent teaching of the doctrine of the Trinity." But I cannot verify the incident.

this kind would have impeded it. Besides which, would you not say that He confined Himself to telling people things which they did not know, but principles which were understood, like that of elementary fair-dealing, He left alone.

B. Perfectly true; and in this He was singularly unlike the great prophets of the Old Testament. Much might be said on that unlikeness. They had a revelation vouchsafed to them of God's Love and a vision of a Deliverer to come. Yet they preached social reform. Was not the difference due to this, that Jesus, being Who He was, was not the recipient of a revelation only, but essentially the Revelation Itself; and that His message to mankind was not that they should set their house in order, but that the Love which He exhibited and His tranquil confidence in the middle of what looked like hideous collapse and ruin, were attributes of God Himself. Hence that the pious conjectures of former ages as to God's being good, in our sense of the word, were borne out and confirmed.

F. I partly understand. But is that thought not rather away from our subject.

B. You are right. Only there is this connexion. As our Lord's vision of truth was quite unclouded, and universal as compared with that of the prophets, on that very account He was satisfied with stamping it deeply on the minds of men. So we who have inherited it are the heirs of His method. We must plant it and let it bear its own fruit in its own time.

F. Yes; those points are worth thinking over. But still don't forget my difficulty. If ordinary plain-headed men like myself had been alive in those days, you don't mean, do you, that He would have taught us doctrine?

B. Let us consider this. The question you ask brings me to my second point, the evidence of the New Testament. By confining myself to the very beginnings of Church History, I have not strayed beyond the New Testament so far; and before I pass on to our Lord's method of teaching, let me sum up what I have been trying to say, as follows:—

The work of Jesus Christ as well as His teaching planted truths in men's minds with unexampled power: truths which were either new or had become blurred. These He committed to a Society, which was divinely strengthened for the tremendous task of passing them on to mankind at large. They did so, and as a result a new type of character came into being, and great social improvements began to be conceived and started; but throughout, and especially when the new life was most vigorous, men's minds were far more set on the *spiritual* change which they had to announce than on the practical changes which were to follow. I would say also that had it been otherwise the practical changes would not have followed, or at least would have been inferior, more earthly, more superficial than they were. Of course it is possible to argue *ad infinitum* over such a statement as that; but with your permission I propose to leave it with you as being worth consideration, and so far unassailable that it ought to be taken as a principle of conduct for all who, like you and me, hold that the Christian message is true.

Now may we proceed to some passages in the Gospel which bear closely upon the matter in hand?

F. Certainly. That is just what I should desire.

B. Well, then, if we ask ourselves what Christ's general attitude towards His hearers might be expected to be, on the assumption, that is, that He was primarily concerned with planting a certain idea of God in men's hearts, we should expect the answer to be that He estimated men chiefly by their receptivity. And in a sense how true this is! How constantly He dwelt on the necessity of Faith, its power in human life, and the impoverishment of all high endeavour without it! But I would have you notice that along with this He never failed to stimulate to the utmost man's faculty of firsthand apprehension. I mean that the very last thing Christ wished any follower of His to become was a torpid holder of undigested maxims, a colourless listener to beautiful truths. The beauty of His teaching—if we except the mere outward qualities—really consisted in its penetrating suggestiveness and unique power of stirring thought.

F. Yes, but wait a moment: thought about what? Surely the Sermon on the Mount was a long, practical, or rather moral, discourse dealing with simple subjects for simple men. I admit there are a few passages in His ordinary teaching which might be called mystical, but apart from the Fourth Gospel, which I suppose we must put aside, they do not amount to much. Broadly, the modern view of His work is true. He went about doing good, and teaching truths full of consolation for suffering humanity; then He died a death full of pain and shame, and, to give us a warrant as to His Divinity, rose again from the dead.

B. I don't suppose any one could traverse that statement on the score of its being fundamentally untrue; but incomplete and pitifully jejune it certainly is. We will take the Sermon on the Mount first. You speak of it as simple. I say it is unfathomably deep, in that it places Infinity before us under the aspect of Love. There is no way of understanding its teaching, unless you discern the connexion of ideas, all hung upon the one prevading truth that the Creator of this world is our Heavenly Father Who loves us infinitely. Based on that truth is a certain view of human life, especially of its anxieties, which we must try to acquire. It is a view which experience shows to be profoundly satisfying and suggestive of hope and progress and growth and of all that is provocative of joy; but only if its theological . . . element is borne in mind throughout. For any one who starts from the commonplace view that man need not fash himself about anything mystic, but should just stick to his duty and vaguely hope for the best, it is a supremely unsatisfying discourse. It touches upon a few ethical subjects, but in a most paradoxical fashion, and, broadly, may be said to leave alone all modern problems altogether. I suggest to you that all Christ's teaching is of this character. It is full of profound sympathy with ordinary humanity, so much so that it is occasionally humorous; it culls its illustrations from the most homely objects and actions, and there is something attractive in it, especially for men of a somewhat rustic unspoilt habit of mind. But along with this, it is practically valueless, unless the hearer allows his soul to be lifted up to a certain view of God, which it consistently assumes and reveals.

F. Well, but what about such a text as "By their fruits ye shall know them"? I take it Christ is there insisting on the cardinal fact that religion without practical effect on life is a vain thing—which is just what I have always believed.

B. Yes; that is true, but note how in the very figure employed my contention is corroborated. Fruits suggest, or ought to, the root, the soil, the stem and branches of the tree. It is perfectly true that if the principles of life are drawn from above, they shall be *known* by the outward effect they produce on earth; but it is equally true that to consider the fruits as superior or more interesting, or more important than the other constituents of a tree, is profoundly and undeniably a wrongheaded way of going to work. In connexion with the intellectual facing of deep problems presented to us on earth and recognized by their vital importance, there is one passage of most searching significance. Do you remember when the Lord asked the leaders of the Jews whether the Baptism of John was from heaven or of men?

F. To be sure.

B. Why did He ask that question?

F. Oh, I suppose it was a convenient way out of a dilemma. They had just asked Him a question to which there was manifestly no answer, and with startling readiness He propounded one which they were equally unable to cope with, and so the situation was saved.

B. But, do you mean that any conundrum would have suited His purpose? or must it not have been connected with the subject under discussion?

F. Well, I suppose it must. Else they would have refused to be drawn aside from their own question.

B. Certainly; and if we seize hold of that fact to begin with, we shall reach a truth of very precious import to us all. There must have been something not only inwardly germane to the main matter in Christ's question but something which they could feel to be appropriate and relevant. Under no other conviction could they possibly have placed themselves in a humiliating position before the people. The Lord was challenged to declare His credentials. He could not have done so without being totally misunderstood by coarse and narrow minds, and it was one of the occasions when a drawing into the light of the treasures of the Kingdom would have been resented by the hearers who understood their preciousness, but would have increased the guilt of the others who ought to have understood it but did not; so with His usual mastery over the situation, He used a question as a way of indicating the truth, but only for those who could sink below the surface.

F. I don't see how He indicated any answer to the question.

B. Ah! but think of this. The truth which He indicated to them was not that which they had asked, but the highest which they were capable of receiving; that is to say, He unveiled to them the moral reason why their growth in knowledge of truth had been arrested, and this of course it was absolutely vital to them to know.

F. Please explain.

B. You see there had been in their experience a really critical challenge offered to them, which was sure to manifest in the case of each one of them his readiness, or the reverse, to lay hold of the divine teaching. Such an event as the ministry of John the Baptist left no one who heard of it quite in the same mental condition as before. It was so startling, so totally unlike anything connected with the ordinary routine of events, that any one, capable of interpreting anything, must have felt powerfully drawn towards the problem of finding its meaning, and forming an estimate of it, which would relate it to other events in human history. Whatever else a sensible man might safely ignore, this was not to be ignored.

F. Was that so?

B. Undoubtedly. Think of the special character of the Baptist's claims. After centuries of quiescence, the prophetic voice had waked again, not timidly or with hesitation, but with all the old fire and confidence, ringing through Palestine the quintessence of the Old Testament message—sin and repentance, judgment to come, and the cleansing of social life. But more: he, a single teacher, had warned the whole people to abase themselves, an intolerably uncongenial summons, one would have thought; but so masterful, so penetrating was that voice, that thousands flocked to hear him, and receive the symbolical cleansing at his hands. Yet he only claimed to be a preparer of Another's way, a herald. Now both in what he taught and what he foretold, he was a great figure, "a burning and a shining light," according to many; and those who took the opposite view, were bound to denounce him as an impostor and a braggart without credentials. Now please notice. Mediocre men may be neglected. We are not called upon to pass any sentence upon them; indeed, we are forbidden to do so. But no sooner does any man's moral stature rise plainly above the ordinary, no sooner does his message claim to come from "no earthly pole," than it is incumbent on every thinking man to form a judgment, and instead of the highest obedience to Christ lying in silence, it becomes the plainest disobedience not to speak. That was the disobedience of which the rulers of the Jews were then guilty.

F. Yes, but you forget the awkwardness of their position. The Temple was full of high-spirited Galileans who had gathered for the Festival, and if the Scribes had uttered their real thoughts, they would have raised a tumult and lost all their influence, probably, with the people.

B. In other words, they turned from their first duty because they were afraid to be honest. But observe: I am not indicting them so much for their refusal to speak out on this particular occasion, as for being totally unable, at the beginning, either to gainsay or to divert the current of popular feeling about John. There must have been a time when the people were undecided and looked to the Scribes for guidance; when the latter did what they could to damp the ardour of the masses for the wonderful Prophet, but finding they could not prevail, they stifled their feelings, or at least kept them secret, gave no lead, expressed no opinion, though they scorned and detested the man who spoke unflinchingly of them, of their falseness, cowardice and bigotry. From the very beginning they feared the people. In other words, they missed their great opportunity of becoming learners, because they were morally cowards. Truth often comes to the human soul in pain, and these men to avoid the pain turned away from her.

F. How do you mean "pain"?

B. Why, the pain of recognizing their own sinfulness. As of yore in the wilderness, and again during the opulent days of Jeroboam II, and at other times, the Jews were besotted with self-satisfaction, and the great preacher came to rouse them from deep spiritual torpor. The heart of the people was so far sound that his reverberating tones found an echo there. But all that the religious leaders of the nation could make of it was that the teaching of repentance was unworthy of the chosen people, or at least of themselves, who knew the law and were scrupulous in its practice. So, on some pretext or other, we know not what, they condemned the Baptist and his message, but were afraid to take up a position of open hostility to him; they left the question unresolved, never considering it fairly and squarely: "Is this man a preacher of righteousness sent by God, even as the prophets of old whose tombs we have built? If not, why not?"

F. Dear me! I never thought of that part of the story. It must of course have been difficult for them. Yet in some ways they were good men. They were zealous about what they thought to be important.

B. True enough. Men as a rule prefer to take abundant trouble of a routine kind rather than sit down and resolutely think whether it isn't all misdirected. The Scribes having lost the idea of a living God, had lost also the true ideal of conduct. Hence they had nothing whereby to compare their ordinary lives, and so were debarred from any feeling of penitence. It is the most commonplace story imaginable, except that the appeal to their better selves was astonishingly vivid, and so their spiritual sloth must have been all the deeper. In their refusal to accept individual responsibility for sin we can see their impenetrability to the teaching of Ezekiel.

F. Well, but was there any particular punishment for this conduct?

B. The punishment, which perhaps seemed to the worldly hearted of the day as nothing, is contained in the terrible sentence "Neither tell I you by what authority I do these things." Jesus refused to give further light to men of darkened hearts, when the first illumination had only made them afraid. A misuse of the great opportunity of learning obviously unfitted them for further teaching. They could not have understood the simplest answer to their own hypocritical question. Just as the reward of faithful service is enlarged responsibility, so the punishment for refusing to think is a withholding of light.

F. What, then, do you exactly infer from this story as to the subject of our talk?

B. Clearly this: that in our religious and moral experience things occur which are intended to evoke from us renewed efforts after truth, clearness of vision, self-abasement, and, in short, a drawing nearer to God. If we are faithful in our answer to the challenge, then we go through a preparation for another challenge, more searching and larger in scope, but similar in its demand on the conscience, and in its stern claim that we must not, in the presence of the Eternal God, trust in our own righteousness.

F. I begin to see. You would, in short, use the incident in order to press home the requirement made upon me, and those of like temperament, not to be content with a service of outward action while refusing to think and study and pray. It may be, you mean, that our outward zeal is only a cloak for the overmastering spiritual indolence, and, for us, involves less effort in reality.

B. Less effort and far less self-abasement. But consider the *à fortiori* aspect of the case. In our religious experience we have witnessed a Greater than John the Baptist; and if the melancholy punishment I have mentioned fell upon a generation which turned from the task of interpreting the Forerunner, what will happen to those who when asked about the Master Himself can only say: We cannot tell?

F. I confess there is much to think over in what you say. But let us take some further teaching in the Gospel to speak about.

B. There is so much, that the difficulty is to know where to begin. But we may generalize to this extent that our Lord was especially emphatic against the very common tendency to draw the line in the matter of spiritual endeavour and say "thus far and no further; if I reach this point I have done enough." There are many indications that He regarded this habit of mind as quite fatal. So, no doubt, did St. Paul when he spoke of "forgetting the things that are behind," etc., and the poet who sang "they will go from strength to strength." Perhaps one of the most telling is the incident of the rich young man. It would be difficult to imagine a plainer verdict upon the tone of mind which refuses to face principles, or rather, to think out bravely whither they lead. Both in this case and in that of the Baptist, we are reminded that there is a kinship, so to speak, between the righteousness of the Old Testament and that of the New Testament. The teaching of the Baptist was meant to make men ready for Christ. So "all these have I kept from my youth up." Those words are not contradicted nor set aside, but their issue is pointed out. Obedience to Moses, in other words, was meant to prepare for the life of faith, by encouraging the sense of need, the conviction of weakness, and other feelings which Christ required before He could speak uplifting words. If that obedience had wrought its full effect on the young man, he would have recognized that now the life of conformity to God's Law was to be enriched by the renunciation of a personal devotion. "Sell, give, and follow Me." Here we have the very opposite of the spirit which asks "Lo, we have left all and followed Thee: what shall we have therefore?"

F. Interesting, no doubt; but I don't quite see the application to the difficulty before us.

B. Well, we must grasp the principle on which Christ acted, leaving on one side what is peculiar to the individual. The man had adopted a certain standard of conduct and fulfilled it adequately, as he supposed. The point of the story is, not whether the standard was adequately or inadequately fulfilled, but the nature of the standard chosen, which was briefly that of the less thoughtful and more conventional people of the time. Similarly a man like yourself is almost bound, if he has generous impulses, to adopt a standard, which is necessarily that of convention, and which holds out a hope of adequate fulfilment; because he has made up his mind that some peculiarity of temperament, is required if a more spiritual or less human standard is to be preferred. Just as the young ruler could say truly "All these have I kept," so you can say truly, "In default of anything higher or richer, I set before myself the idea of benefiting my countrymen, in a sphere too much neglected in the past, viz. that of linking the various Dominions of the British Empire together in a grand league of self-defence, and as a bulwark against the horrible devastation of modern warfare for all time. I have done the work as well as a man can. What lack I yet?"

F was silent for a moment, and then said, Wait a bit: my aim has not been conventional, because as you justly say this particular sphere of work has been neglected in the past.

B. I mean conventional in the sense that countless swarms of good-hearted men and women nowadays throw themselves into social service, to avoid the pain of thinking whether it is really what they were sent into the world to do. You may have chosen a comparatively new sphere, but none the less it is characterized, as all the others are, by being engrossing first, then by aiming at the material betterment of our secular life, in other words, at peace founded on material self-interest, and so far it shares with other social aims a grievous uncertainty whether it will ultimately do more good than harm. Yet for the nonce it has all the appearance of offering an unassailably sound line of effort.

F. Good gracious! you say the work is chosen for being safe, and yet is profoundly uncertain in its results. What do you mean?

B (*after a pause*). I find it difficult to put this shortly, and am afraid of taxing your patience. First, in what sense do I speak of your work as safe? I mean that its professed object is certain to be approved of by all safe and respectable people of the day. It is thought a thoroughly worthy object, so worthy and so difficult that it sets many pulses beating quicker as soon as they hear of it. Unusual though it be, it is not an inch beyond the average opinion of the age in which we live. Thus any one can choose it without patiently facing for himself what the issues of his life really are. He finds an ideal ready to hand.

F. Very well. And now about the uncertainty.

B. Have you ever asked yourself how many of the great changes or conscious efforts towards progress, that have been made in history, have accomplished the thing at which they were aimed? Certainly the reverse of the question would give some strange answers. You and I would agree that, considering what Christianity is, anything that prepared the way for it must be considered a mighty blessing among mankind. But many of these preparations were calamities at the time, borne, it is true, mainly by one nation, the Jews. For instance, if one thinks over the crisis of the young Church in Jerusalem, described in Acts xv., it becomes clear that had the Jewish party been much stronger or much narrower than it was,

Christianity would have been throttled in its cradle. But what chiefly prevented it from being stronger was the influence of the Diaspora. Now the Diaspora was largely due to the harrying of the Israelites by the Assyrians, and the Captivity; events which must have worn the appearance of unmitigated calamities. Broadly speaking, also, I would say that where mankind has accomplished an object which has had beneficent results, those results were not the ones intended. For instance, the spreading of the Greek language was a mighty assistance to St. Paul; but in so far as it was caused by the efforts of Alexander, we may say it was brought about by a man who in accomplishing it, was aiming at the spread of the Greek spirit, not at the spread of Christianity. The Romans, too, established the Pax Romana; but they were aiming, not at helping Christianity by free intercourse between peoples round the Mediterranean, but because they desired a quiet life. So in the general hurly-burly of civilization, the condition of affairs is far too complex for any one to foresee the exact effects of great movements. Yet many of them have been wildly applauded when they were first undertaken because they seemed to be in accord with what we call the spirit of the age; in other words, to be the kind of effort most in favour with the thoughtless majority of living people.

F. Possibly you are right in the matter of great political changes and the like. But what about the philanthropies of the day?

B. It is almost more of a commonplace that the "best laid plans" of kindly hearted men and women do harm more often than good. For instance, there are theories, not easily disproved, in vogue among modern Darwinians, that even the great increase in temperance among English people will be found to be productive of terrible harm, in the sense that it prevents Nature from eliminating from the stock the deleterious elements of alcohol-fever; because there is only one way of preventing alcoholism from being transmitted, that is, by its unmarried victims drinking themselves to death. Hence the increase of sobriety on which we plume ourselves to-day may be merely the storing up of vicious tendencies, which after a few generations have passed will break out with refreshed malignity and work havoc.[1] Now, for my part, I can hardly believe that any one is in a position to prove, or even to believe, this theory; but its very promulgation is an indication that we are coming to believe in our most successful efforts either bringing about some unexpected good results, or some equally unexpected bad ones.

F. I must interpose here. You indict social effort on two grounds, first for being in accordance with public opinion, secondly for being incalculable in its effects. Of course, the second is a profoundly dangerous doctrine; for if it gets about, it must paralyse all effort whatever. But I will recur to that presently. As to the first, I don't see the objection that because a man's career is approved by contemporary public opinion therefore it is wrong, especially if your second count is allowed. If all careers, programmes, plans and organizations are incalculable, why not let a young man be guided by public opinion? *Parmi les aveugles*, etc. To go back to Scripture, do you find much warrant for this particular view?

B. Of course the Gospels are full of warnings against the guidance of public opinion. But I would like you to

[1] This depressing theory is advocated by Mr. and Mrs. Whetham in the *Hibbert Journal*, Oct. 1911.

consider exactly the epithet "safe" and what it means in this connexion. When a man lays his plans for life they seem to him safe in proportion as they are approved by public opinion; and public opinion always approves of those that seem likely not to end in failure, but in establishing some result thought to be desirable. Others that demand original thought, and are out of the fashion of the time, are held to be insecure and risky. Now without affirming that quite all those that are held to be risky are in reality the safest, I find that the converse is true, viz. that those held to be safe, ultimately lead to results neither desired nor expected. The others have this that is good in them: they depend not on the approval of the unthinking majority, but on their congruity to something ideal, or anyhow not common. They reach out into mystery; they demand a venture, and they seem to exercise continually the noblest faculties of a man's being. And in their results—well, I will recur to them later. But first tell me if this description does not remind you of a tremendous passage in the Gospel?

F. I am afraid not. Do tell me.

B. In the Parable of the Talents, the man who buried his one talent in the earth is the type of the safe man, i.e. one who starting with certain premisses into which he does not inquire, suits his conduct to them quite consistently, but yet is condemned with a terrible severity at the end of the story. Now in giving you what I conceive to be the right explanation of the parable, I hope you will not mind my drawing the condemned character in colours suggested by the lives of men who try to live on a creed which consists wholly of Duty, but banishes what they call mysticism or dogma.

F. Never mind that. The picture seems paradoxical

enough, as of all people the duty-doing man is least like the man who shirked his duty altogether. At least, so one would suppose.

B. To begin with, then, this person behaves in an unaccountably stupid manner. The coin he receives is only valuable if it is used boldly, or (if it is artfully worked) if it be stored in a glass case to be looked at. Now the man knew one thing about it, and apparently nothing else. He was aware that it was precious. But the condemnation would not have been added, if he had been merely ignorant or stupid, or both together, neither would those very common qualities have induced him to act with such uncommon ineptitude. There was a deep principle on which he acted, and which explains all. He took a wrong view of his master, conceiving of him as a hard man set on demanding more than could be given, whereas he ought to have known that he was just and gracious. That, consistently acted on, is the key to his conduct. Any trading with the coin seemed to involve a certain risk; and risk is just what he could not face, when there was the master's return to be waited for. So he treated the coin in accordance with the general idea that it was precious, but in a way to contradict its very nature.

F. Well, that is interesting and may be right; what about the application?

B. We Christians have received something precious, viz. the Holy Spirit of God. It is a gift about which many know nothing, except that it is vaguely precious, and they conceive of God as a taskmaster who has given them far too little for them to venture with and reach forth and use, so as to make something glorious out of life; they persuade themselves they have not the resources for anything higher than abstaining from squandering their gift on evil-living. So they bury it, or as St. Paul puts it, they "quench" it.[1] They fashion their lives on some humdrum routine principle, forgetting that the beautiful living thing given to them, if not constantly exercised, dies within them, and all the time they flatter themselves on their consistency and uprightness, little knowing how unutterable is their loss, or how grievously wrong their starting-point. For their starting-point is the tremendous lie propagated sedulously and with devilish skill by the father of lies, that God is a hard Taskmaster who has provided His own with too little for that which He requires. In proportion as your duty religionist, so to call him (I mean the man who restricts his allegiance to his conscience and the demands of the moral law), succeeds in banishing from his creed and his thoughts and preoccupations the idea of a living, loving God, in so far he is assimilated to this poor fellow who thought he was doing the one sensible thing open to him by burying the bright gold coin in the soil. He is striving to live the loveless life, after the life of venture for the love of God has been revealed to him by the example of others and by the story of Jesus. Of course, many men rise above their professed creed, and wherever you find in the work of people who cannot say a word about their fundamental convictions, that spring of energy and hopefulness and humility, which bespeaks the Christian saint, it is because they have been enabled to substitute, perhaps unconsciously, the life of faith for the life of works; that is to say, they will speak to you only of duty and her stern decrees, but in their hearts there is glowing the personal love of God Himself; because their single-mindedness makes them apt learners and quick recipients. Only, they are lame and hesitating as teachers

[1] 1 Thess. v.

in that they cannot readily pass on to their children what has been to them

> the fountain-light of all their day,

or even indicate its Source. Thus some are saved from the starved and barren life; but otherwise, if they are consistent with their intellectual beliefs, they cannot trade with the talent; they lack all element of venture and living confidence, and when they are bidden to rise out of the rut of fashion they fail to hear the appeal, and one more opportunity of fruitfulness passes by for ever, because they think they will be able to say to God the *Dator Munerum*, "Lo! there Thou hast what is Thine," when they try to return the unused, unexercised gift of divine life, and it has perished into the semblance of a gold coin covered with mould.

F. And what would you say, then, about the two "good and faithful" servants who brought back the ten and five talents to their lord?

B. They are those who start with the unalterable conviction that their God-given resources are enough for the demands that will be made upon them; because the Gospel story has taught them that they can securely trust their Heavenly Father. So, instead of letting themselves believe that religion is for a minority of people of a peculiar temperament, they "press forward"; they hear of holy men and heroes who are not afraid to venture their heavenly treasure, especially as they find at once that, every time they use it, it grows, and no matter what claim is made upon it there is always abundance to go on with.

F. Yet, I gather, in such a case as my own, for instance, you wouldn't say that my career was mistaken, and ought to be changed for something more definitely ministerial?

B. No, not at present, anyhow. But if you can bear in mind more constantly and with a deeper sincerity and vividness, Whose are the resources with which you are equipped, and to Whom the returns will some day be made, there will be vastly more life in your work and, above all, you will be prepared against failure.

F. Failure ! But why think of such a thing ? Surely, if the definite Christian is anything he is hopeful ; that is to say, he refuses to contemplate his life's work as failing.

B. Woe to him, then, if he sets his hope on what we call success. That is one of the awful facts in the policy of burying the talent : it never brings a man up short against the fact of failure. Now think of the solemn words in the Parable of the Sower : "And when the sun was up they were scorched." They indicate the kind of experience against which we can only be prepared by having the roots of our lives planted deep. I mean the experience of finding all human maxims inapplicable, all the sympathy of friends either a hollow pretence or quite unavailing to heal. Then it is that the religion of duty is like a husk for a hungry man to eat.

F. But only a minority, I should say, undergo any such trial.

B. It is not uncommon to see the smooth, quiet life broken in upon by sickness or loss or bereavement. Sun scorchings of one sort or another seem to be the rule in every case where work of real durable value has been done; that is to say, some grievous obstacle has been overcome. The youth starts with his heart aflame and his hopes high, but before long he finds himself praised and blamed just for the wrong things, and whenever he is vitally eager and sees a little further than other people, the Titanic bulk of human stupidity rears itself against him, and he is derided and misunderstood. Or in his home affections he is thwarted most dismally, or his health, without breaking down, makes it extremely difficult for him to exert himself beyond the point of a jog-trot performance of routine. But beyond all these, is the corroding scepticism which threatens to invade all modern work: *cui bono*? Now tell me, against such blighting influences as these what has your duty-lover to set?

F. It is not easy for one like me to say; but surely you do see cases of men triumphantly surviving all these buffetings, and keeping the spring of their energy active to the last, far on into old age.

B. Again, I say, by their fruits the trees show when they are deeply rooted. It is impossible for any one to take up his cross and follow Christ, without a deep feeling for His love, though they may not be able to express it.

F. I must admit that there is something in what you say, and if only I met more men who obviously gain life and strength from giving their minds to the great mystic fact of God's Love, I should feel quite decidedly that my own life had been impoverished by far too little of such elements as Prayer, Meditation and Communion. But now let me put plainly to you the grand difficulty on which you have touched once or twice, as to hopefulness in spite of scepticism and failure, because I am come to the time of life when hope, to be worth much, must have something to feed on, and I long to know if your way of looking at things will enrich my resources at all.

B. The subject is vastly important, so pray explain yourself.

F. Well, you see, after knocking about as I have for many years, working for something like Imperial Federation in our Empire, one gains a pretty good knowledge of certain things : the vast importance of the question, and the equally vast difficulties in the way of effecting anything really adequate to the emergency with which we are confronted. It is apparent to me that the Dominions are drifting either to complete independence of England, or to some form of Federal Union ; but various obstacles in the way of the latter are so formidable that I am coming to the conclusion that it will never be brought about. But complete independence means the end of the Empire, and very possibly the absorption of vast tracts of territory, over which the British flag now waves, into the hands of alien powers. This prospect disheartens me altogether, and I have often wished that I had the kind of temperament men call optimistic, so that I might interpret these facts in a somewhat less dismal fashion. Now, to come to the point, would you say that a change of the religious point of view in the direction which you are advocating would afford any hope of such a "lift" in my mental horizon ? One hears that a thorough believer in Christianity is sure to be a hopeful man. Is this so ?

B. If you mean that a thoroughly Christian spirit would enable a man to ignore the difficulties, and to anticipate a more successful end to your particular labours, the answer is a decided negative. I mean, of course, "successful" in the usual sense.

F. Then in what way is it true that the Christian religion brings hopefulness with it ? If it is not optimistic in that ordinary sense, it might be compatible with pessimism.

B. No. It ought not to be difficult to draw a distinction between being ready to anticipate failure, and being prepared to see failure work for good. For instance, suppose all attempts at Imperial Federation seem likely to fail; the duty-religionist is likely to despair unless he has principles in the back of his mind, which he has borrowed from some creed other than what he professes. But a true Christian temper would encourage the hope that this failure would work for good by strengthening the fibre of the people: making each country rely more than ever on itself, and so forth. Also, previously to failure it would be unwilling to abandon hope, because it would see and probably evoke sympathies in needful quarters, where the more prosaic and less ardent spirit would not descry them.

F. Then you mean that in two ways, hopefulness is shown by those who enter into the Christian temper as some certainly do: first by refusing to abandon belief in the good feeling of those who must co-operate; secondly, by falling back on a theory that if all else fails, the very discipline of failure will do good. But is the first of these two a matter of religious belief? I should have thought it was a purely temperamental quality of sympathy.

B. Undoubtedly the inclination to believe that others are sympathetic differs in individuals according to their temperament; but that is not the same thing as saying that religion has nothing to do with it. Whatever supply of such inclination religion may find, it will quicken and invigorate it. But it is a very obscure question.

F. No doubt, and less important for our discussion than the other which concerns the power of hope outlasting failure. But it is still a mystery to me how any religious belief or emotional susceptibility can be proof against failure which depresses beyond a certain point; and I can't help thinking that many men would agree with me if they spoke their minds freely. Let me put the case to you without disguise—the melancholy case of this great country of ours. Supposing any one like myself on cool reflection convinced himself that all this splendid accumulation of wealth, splendour, manliness and beauty, and qualities which have conquered the world is to "dissolve" under the long, slow corrosion of internal decay "and like the baseless fabric of a vision, leave not a rack behind," the question is not whether he can just fend off from himself utter despair and "wretchlessness," but whether this fending off does not become impossible to him in proportion as he has devoted himself wholeheartedly to his duty. Who are they who do good work in the world? Are they not just those whose hopes, as well as energy, are wholly set on the task in hand? Real, eager self-dedication to a great cause, a conviction even if exaggerated, of the overwhelming importance of the undertaking; these are the ingredients which go to the building up of a firm fabric, instead of the showy tinsel of wood, hay and straw, so often the best to be expected from the workman who is afraid of being narrow and who ends by losing all his force. Now do let us face this question fairly and squarely, aye, and candidly too. For I will admit, and have admitted what is lacking in my own position, and I know you too well to be afraid that you will fob me off with "eristic" subtleties.

I say, then, that when you tell me of your conviction that the very essence of a virtuous, attractive, and fruitful character is a forgetfulness of self in something higher, and that that something higher is the life of God, revealed and imparted to man as he sinks himself into it as a recipient—for this I take to be your meaning—I have before me the picture of a character more contemplative than active; more of the Mary than the Martha in it;

and without disputing the Gospel verdict that it is the "better part" to choose, I yet affirm that to many men it is a sealed book. Further, that to those very men the finest, most single-minded, most self-forgetful of all types of life is the life of unselfish activity, be it in a small domestic circle, or in the larger world of public affairs; and that, looked at impartially, the real work of the world is done by such men more than by others. Again, that if these men made a conscientious attempt to change themselves from Marthas into Marys, they would be, in reality, spoiling themselves; not living the life which to them is truly natural; that is God-prescribed; and in so doing they become actors or "hypocrites," that is to say, they lose the genuineness, the driving force and effectiveness which belong to simplicity; in short they are born for one thing and aim at another.

B. You interest me profoundly. Will you go on to state the practical difference between the two? I mean that, granting your premisses there will be a difference, of course, in those matters where the active passes into the contemplative life, or *vice versa.*

F. To be sure. Let us then be frank. A man of strenuous activity cannot be what is called a man of prayer. Prayer is not his *métier*; he is constituted to give himself to his profession, and in proportion as he does so wholeheartedly, he works to some purpose. It is right for him to say his prayers, and if he has time, let him read the Bible; but if you demand more of him, you will be urging him to spoil his nature by trying to be what he is not; and to go through life pacing in time to some one else's tune, like a horse decked out in fine trappings for a royal funeral. So much for the loss involved if the wrong man tries to be too religious. But if this summary is to be complete, I will not conceal what I have already admitted: there is a huge defect in the active non-contemplative life, which, it may be, though I am not sure, the other life escapes, viz. that when pain and disappointments, thwartings and annoyances reach a certain pitch of intensity and frequency and permanence, there are no resources to meet them which do not dwindle away as youth and buoyancy fail. On the one hand, then, I find myself unable to feel quite content about the Gospel, because it seems to demand a kind of life which to me is unnatural; on the other hand, if I try, simply and loyally to live up to the light I have received, I have to own that when the real unavoidable pinch of life's trial begins, when the keen knife of sorrow, error, and failure makes its first stabs in the soul, my equipment fails; what is the way out of this?

B. Well, of course, the answer to that question would depend partly on the nature of the trial which had to be faced. Could you indicate it more clearly?

F. In my own case, I am sorry to say there is no difficulty in doing that. It is not a personal matter but concerns humanity at large. Think of the gradual sundering of our Empire, and what that means. Grand settlements of our kith and kin in different parts of the earth ready, by inclination, by loyalty, by self-interest, even, to knit together the different countries into a Union which would be powerful enough to maintain the peace of the whole civilized world, are now inertly and timidly eyeing their position, blocking proposals and feebly trying to cater for the local popular cry whatever it may be. So at least it appears to me, and the more I look into the constitutional and financial aspect of this huge question, the more it is borne in upon me that nothing but a mighty wave of unselfish patriotism and statesmanlike feeling will ever surmount the terrible obstacles, and that there is no evidence of such influences being operative at the present day. Therefore, what hope can I form of the future of the English-speaking peoples? Without some powerful bond knitting them together what are their resources against gradual dissolution or rapid conquest? The answer to that question is dismal indeed. The social problems in Western Europe gather complexity every year, and every year there is more effort made to grapple with them. Along with this immense display of vitality, there is a great outburst of intelligent effort for national improvement, wider culture, spreading of interest in every direction, and increased intellectual vivacity in all classes. But with it all, and undermining it all, is the hideous fact of the decline of the birth-rate in all the progressive, best-educated sections of society; not the governing classes alone, but in every section and class which gives evidence of any real eagerness to make themselves and the world round them better. Tremendous, and nothing short of it, though the dangers encompassing us are, I verily believe we should face them all and with God's help come off victorious, if it weren't that the very men and women with the stamina, the brains and character to deal with them, are not being produced. The decline began in 1875. We are beginning to feel the want of young men with the power of leaders in every profession; and we have a long period of impoverishment before us, even if we came to our senses at once, but history gives no evidence of any nation going back on its tracks when once it has taken to this dark and fatal path. Meantime we are draining our resources more and more; pouring the best young lives more and more rapidly into the Civil Service, and demanding an ever-increasing number for Colonial posts. And nobody has a remedy to suggest. It is horrible to think of living and trying to work in a dying community; to see the splendid material of young lives diminishing in number steadily, remorselessly every year; and above all, to believe that the irresistible evil is due principally to a love of ease and shrinking from responsibility, which is corroding the old English strength and grit. Can any trial be greater to bear? It would be nothing if one put pleasure first and patriotism second; but, to one, who loves England and believes she has a grand part to play in the development of humanity, could any trial, I repeat, be harder to bear?

B (*after a pause*). Ah! my dear friend, I feel for you. You are one of a large number nowadays who feel these things, and are well-nigh succumbing to the burden of spiritual depression. You do not, however, wish me to discuss how far I agree in your outlook, or look forward to some recovery before it is too late, or think that the anxieties are bracing to the national character. Let us leave all these on one side, and assuming that the gloomier forecast is reasonable, turn our best attention to the central question, which has, in different forms, occupied us all this long and delightful walk. It is this. A believer in Christianity, but not from emotion, nor what is ordinarily called a religious man, or inclined to the contemplative side of life, learns that while there may be some upholding power in religion in the face of trials like this, there is certainly none without it. Is it possible to explain how far and in what manner a bright and vivid faith in the great truths of Christianity would help, when a merely intellectual assent to the propositions is powerless to aid?

F. Yes, that is exactly it.

B. Then let me say first that the very putting of the question shows a lack not of mental perception at all, but of spiritual experience, and I trust you will not take that expression to mean some vague and cloudy transport of the mind, untranslatable and incommunicable, but a definite interpreting of certain data with the highest faculties of our being. Broadly speaking, you would not be puzzled for a moment if you really knew what is meant by communion with God; because certain truths which to you now are unreal, would then become living and certain. Such as for instance, "A thousand years in Thy sight are but as yesterday, seeing that is past as a watch in the night." Without meditation, silent hours, and in short, spiritual experience, few men can take in the wonder of the patience of God; the slowness of His advance, the immense length of His preparation-epochs, the glory of His future unveiling. But it might be clear even to the intellect alone, that when these expressions cease to be mere words, all the great issues of life assume a new colour and we are no longer dealing with the same problem. "'My ways are not as your ways,' saith the Lord," are words which were wrung out of some deep experience, and expressed what the speaker literally had learnt as a vivid certainty. Now this sort of knowledge is the illumination of the facts of life by the Holy Spirit working on a man's mind, till the illumination becomes his own. But man's chief part in the process is the conscious and repeated acts of communion with God; made in the confidence that they will maintain him in participation with the divine life. If any such expressions convey a truth, are you not in danger of practically denying it when you look on it as questionable whether such communion can produce the effect you desiderate, and also of forgetting what a part it played in the earthly life of our Lord?

F. When I think of what you say, I can imagine a kind of vision irradiating our earthly life, but as soon as I turn my eyes towards the prospect of decay and the collapse of high endeavour, the old depression returns.

B. No doubt it does. Do you suppose that a spiritual communion with the Eternal God can be started straight off after the neglect of years? and that its effects can be perceptible at once, when from the nature of things they must come slowly and in ways hard to describe?

F. Will you go on then, and tell me some more?

B. There is this ingredient of an intellectual kind, viz. the perspective in the view taken of evil and its place in the world. If your prognostication of events is approximately correct, we have to look forward to that which seems to our clearest sight a great set back in the history of mankind: the failure of the English Empire to do its work of civilizing and evangelizing the backward races: a failure exemplified by that of not saving the kaffirs in Africa from Islamism. Now we assume that this is going to happen, and it will be what we call an evil. The truest Christian philosophy is to regard it as one of the great instances of a stage in the history of mankind, which we have to fight against and arrest if possible, but which we may be perfectly certain will in the long run work for good; yet the duty of arresting it is potently clear and binding on us all.

F. That is all very well; but it surely contradicts all reason.

B. Doubtless, if reason, and such operations of our thinking faculty as could be rationally described, were all we had to trust to, we should be enmeshed in a huge net of puzzle and bewilderment. As it is, we have to recognize the limitation of our ordinary thought, and the certainty that there is an infinite realm beyond, about which our mental faculties can tell us nothing; yet something in us tells us something. For instance: our Lord indicated this particular difficulty quite clearly in the words, "It must be that offences come; but woe to that man by whom they come." The climax of illustration for these words was given by His own Death and Passion. Some students believe that Judas, seeing the end was inevitable, thought himself justified in bringing it about by betrayal. But we know he was wrong, and would have been wrong, even if he had known that the Death was to be the foundation of hope for countless millions of people. Similarly, if Nicodemus in the Sanhedrin opposed the plan for the capture and murder, he was right, and would have been right whether he knew what the Death meant or not. Surely that is undeniable.

F. Well, I suppose so. But it would be much easier to assent, if one could be sure that Nicodemus did *not* know.

B. True. But that remark hardly applies to Judas, and I should say that as to ignorance often making duty plainer we need not be in any misgiving. I mean in this way. You start the question as to these vast changes in human history, revolutions, decays, failures, conquests, injuries and so forth being matters which a Christian can regard with any hope. I point to the grand failure-triumph of Calvary, and you admit that as long as an individual was not enlightened as to its issue and bearing on mankind's future, he could be under no sort of hesitation beforehand as to preventing it if he could. But we are in just as dark ignorance as to the bearing of these big events on the world's history as Nicodemus was about Calvary. They look to us as if they were fraught with irretrievable disaster, and that is enough reason for our trying to prevent them; and therein lies the difference between Christianity and fatalism. We perhaps may not say it is God's will that our Empire should crumble, though we may be able to feel that out of the melancholy wreckage some glorious fabric shall some day rise. But certainly we can say it is not His will that we should sit idly by while events are portending which seem to us all to be baneful, and which, like Calvary, the best minds of the time cannot interpret in any other way.

F. There is no difficulty about our duty being to stop these horrors if we can, but the puzzle is about warding off despair if we can't.

B. Despair is, of course, often quite reasonable and right for a complete Atheist, if there be such a thing; but it is completely the negation of all belief, as well as reason, for a Theist, and still more so for a Christian. There is a turning of common calamities into blessings which is a wonderful mystery, but it very frequently happens. Take the most wonderful of all. A young man falls into sin and nearly breaks his mother's heart. Years after he meets with an accident, and on his deathbed reveals to her that his fall was the one thing that brought him to a knowledge of God. That is a real experience; but our reason is baffled by it. The instance is relevant, because the terrible part of the trial before us is the conviction that we have brought it on by our own fault. Now, as it is impossible to foresee or imagine the blessed issue of any calamity in ordinary life which is the direct result of sin, gross indifference, studied brutish heartlessness, ruthless ambition, or insensate perversity, so on the vast stage of the world's history, colossal tragedies may be impending, the very thought of which fills us with dismay, and to avert which we are called upon to spend our best efforts and even our last drop of blood. None the less, despair is an immeasurable sin because it is a denial of God, and after all, there is no sin comparable to that in depth of wickedness, malignancy or blindness; to say nothing of its effects on earth.

F. Well, but the effects of this calamity will be very terrible, and I cannot see that however robust may be your belief in God's government of the world, it can alter the dire prospect. After all, awful things have happened, about which not one consoling fact has emerged into view from all the dismal wreckage. I can see no light.

B. Some such words as those must have been used by the Jews when they asked Jesus for a sign. It seems such a natural request; and yet He called them "evil and adulterous" for making it. "Unsound, corrupt, and false to *the* great contract vow." What vow? Why, surely, the vow of union which the nation had long ago made with God, and which they were breaking now because they would not trust Him. As matrimony without mutual affection, so was the relation between the chosen people and Jehovah, when it was devoid of trust. But are you not asking for a sign too? You want some open pledge of reward before you commit yourself to Him. That is what it comes to.

F. No, but one always thinks that the Jews demanded some compelling sign in the sky which should force their belief in Christ.

B. Yes, but forcing belief simply means saving the individuals from the necessity of choosing between trusting or perishing. We are tempted to conceive of a middle course in which the belief in the highest revelation may be exempted from the effort of our whole being. But there is no such thing. Such a belief if it were possible were valueless, a mere husk, an exsiccation, of the real thing, which is a self-committal of the whole being, a yielding of life to life; and that is the only alternative to perishing. "He that loveth his life shall lose it." Or think of another figure. It is wonderful how often our divine Teacher when He is not illustrating truth from childhood, uses some figure connected with marriage or with marriage-banquets. So let us test your position or rather your professed position, in comparison with that which we think of as the religious life, by the figure of marriage. Conceive of marriage under its highest aspect, as, thank God, we still have opportunities of doing in England, when two lives are blended by the power of sanctified natural affection and complemented by joint service and unselfish help. Make it in your mind as near the ideal as you can; and then think what it would become, if either the man or the woman were to say to the other, "I will trust you, but you must first show me a sign that it is worth while." What would happen? Why, the uttermost tragedy of human life, the record of which may be read in any newspaper any morning; when hard logic and selfish common-sense (in this case the same as blindness) are the only response to an unreasoning, undisciplined love, and through bitterness and strife the two lives fall completely asunder into the last stage of infidelity. Not for nothing did our Lord speak of the asking for a sign as the note of an adulterous generation.

F. I think I begin to see. But what about hopefulness?

B. St. Paul's great words about the relation between

Christ and the Church being a mystery like that of marriage—one of the scores of deep sayings in the New Testament, where this precious truth is uttered, revealing the secret of the beauty of home life—will give us the clue to your question. Let us picture as well as we can what the ideal relation would be. On the one side the Lord of Life and Glory creating, sustaining, inspiring and teaching the Society we call the Church ; to which He has committed the one supreme task of renewing the world by perpetually bringing to it His own undying, undecaying Life ; by teaching, by warning, by example, passing on the priceless message of His own redeeming Love. That is the *work* of the Church and the true meaning of all her activities, and it ought to be, of course, the one aim of every individual member throughout the entire Body. Now no sooner do we set ourselves seriously to this task under any one of the countless forms in which we are permitted to undertake it, than we find out the wholly unexpected, novel and most blessed fact, that where we are most truly effective, most fruitful, most Christ-like in our endeavours and our working is often where we have failed most deplorably according to the ordinary human standard of failure. Not quite always, lest too easy a sign should be given, but so as to show us most convincingly that just as the dark and shameful appearance of the drama of Golgotha was simply the appearance to our purblind vision of the glory of the Lord manifested in a world of sin, so if we once learn that lesson we shall discern in the very collapse of our earthly hopes, innocent and child-like though they be, the evidence of our work being " not in vain in the Lord." It is almost beyond question that as things are, that which seems to us to be cruel adversity, or backsliding, or ignominy and collapse, is the very condition of real fruitfulness, the fruitfulness of faithful work; for work so carried on to the end is in truth faithful work. In the power of this living truth hopefulness thrives: it cannot die.

F. You would then say that such thoughts must have been in St. Paul's mind when he said, "We are saved by hope." For my part, I had for long been supposing that the application of those words was in the practical life; a man's work is quickened by hope; but I can hardly think now that the words should be so limited.

B. Certainly not. The Apostle meant the "hope that is not seen." It is literally a saving influence, one of those ingredients in a man's temper which wards off destruction,[1] but only if it be founded, consciously or unconsciously, on the knowledge of God and on confidence in His government of the world. One of the elements in that confidence will be the perception that while all really permanent work is the spreading of God's Kingdom on earth, there is hardly any form of calamity which can for long arrest that work, if only men's wills are quickened to obey. If that is done, all that is good in your schemes will be accomplished; but no collapse need be dreaded because His purpose cannot fail. But all that I have said, which is only a tiny fragment of the possible answer to your question, depends on the deep underlying fact which only experience can teach you, viz. that the power to seize and live on these and similar truths is a gift of the Holy Spirit of God, which is never withheld from those who seek it.

[1] Rom. viii. 24. See Godet in loc. "Hope" in St. Paul's view is a spiritual thing which actualizes the redemption of the world. When Christ accomplished that redemption, it was "in the line of hope."

F. Ah! well; it sounds somehow consoling, and I must think over it all. But doesn't it strike you yourself as a little abstract in presence of huge concrete dangers?

B. I don't deny that I have purposely put the abstract before you, because I know it cannot fail. But in trying to be more concrete we necessarily drop on to a level where uncertainty creeps in. Yet I hold to the hope that in a department of life not ordinarily associated with religion, there are signs of a great advance being made in the general conception of Christian brotherhood and therewith a vigorous effort towards co-operation.

F. Where? How?

B. In the immense world of finance and industry. It can hardly be for no good purpose that the marvellous interdependence of nations each with its need of credit, has come to be a fact. It obviously makes for peace, and predisposes distant people to consider co-operation as favourable to their highest interests.[1] Again there are some very cheering signs in the conduct of huge industries that a higher ethic is being taught us by sharp experience of the terrific failure of the lower. A friend said to me the other day that the hope of society seems to lie in monopolists, because they are becoming so big and so important that they must learn how to serve the community; the community is too much interested in them to allow them to be selfish. I find the same idea worked out in the interesting essay called *Inspired Millionaires*.[2] If we are being taught brotherliness in the weird pagan-looking world of business, may we not

[1] See a most instructive article in the March number of *The Round Table* (175 Piccadilly.)

[2] Stanley Lee. (Grant Richards.)

hope that it will spread far enough to weld together the Dominions of old England?

But, old friend, while we have been talking, the sun has been setting over yon beech copse; and never with greater splendour of passing. What a comment on what we have been thinking! That glory is bringing the divine nearer to many a soul at this moment. But we are told that the colours all depend on dull, disagreeable things, like rain clouds and dust particles floating in the air. So it is that in Oxford Street we can see the most gorgeous sunsets; and I have even heard that their brilliancy and spangled iridescence are more irresistible in their appeal nowadays than ever before; for what reason think you? Because of the dust raised by the motor-cars. How can we despair of anything after that?

F. Well, many thanks to you. I suppose it is time for us to get back to the house.

CHAPTER VIII

Conclusion

IN considering wherein consists the essence of the good character, which is at the same time admirable and attractive, we have been led to recognize that while the absence of Egoism would probably be the broadest designation of character as manifested in life, there is an equally true, though narrower, description given in a positive way by the word Humility. Reflection shows that this quality must have something whereon to rest. In other words a man cannot forget or ignore himself unless he has his affections set on something higher ; and in history we have a clear indication that that higher something is the revelation made to mankind in Christ ; seeing that the recognition of Humility as an essential quality of that which is admirable and lovable in human character was contemporaneous with the first preaching of the Gospel. It was a marked feature of our Lord's teaching, and was enforced in the Apostolic writings in the light of the facts of the Sacrifice on Calvary, the Resurrection from the Dead, and the work of the Holy Spirit after the day of Pentecost.

Humility is not simply a low estimate of self, though it exhibits a freedom from self-assertion, love of display, or desire for fame. A low estimate would often be ridiculous, if once the principle of comparison with others be admitted, and it generally is admitted in proportion as the opposite principle of service to God is feebly grasped. There are characters to which the bare appeal of duty comes with something of divine force, paramount and irresistible; and the offering of self to it is similar in its effects to the self-surrender made in other cases to the Personal God. But the difference is that the religious principle of humble self-surrender can be propagated from generation to generation, while there is nothing in mere loyalty to duty which can be explained to growing minds if once they begin to reflect at all on the basis of conduct. Again, there is the difference that the former, where it is genuine, fosters humility, while the latter, unless it is infused with something of mystery and awfulness which does not logically belong to it, may be thorough, unquestioning and consistent, and yet compatible with pride and egoism. Nor does a bare appeal to duty offer the slightest explanation of the historical fact that Humility only became a recognized virtue in consequence of the work of Christ in the world.

It remains then, for those who feel bound to rate dutifulness far higher than the belief in any doctrine, to weigh well the following consideration: that independently of the overwhelming obligation to embrace and ever hold fast anything which claims successfully to be a revelation from God to man—that is to say, purports to be such for reasons which they cannot overthrow—they ought to give their minds to the connexion between that Revelation and human character.

The reason why many educated people practically ignore Christian doctrine is that they have persuaded themselves that character is everything and doctrine therefore insignificant. But suppose it is shown that the very foundation of all that is most essential, most winning, most fruitful in character, is the outcome of a deeply-rooted belief in the Divine Revelation, the situation in which they are placed is no longer the same. It is open to them as rational beings to adopt one of two courses: either to yearn towards the acceptance of the Revelation in its central teaching of the Love of God, to ask for the gift of the Spirit in Whom it is understood, and so to order their lives that by doing of God's will they may know of the doctrine; or else resolutely to bar all reflection on the principle of the matter and to reverence beauty of character without attempting to understand its basis, merely because its manifestations are passing lovely and pleasant. This last position would allow them to be in a vague unthinking fashion "supporters of religion"; but if they are in any sense of the word Theists, how unspeakably such a way of dealing with the problem flouts all reason! To say nothing of their own inner life and its great need for every possible safeguard against countless forms of egoism; leaving on one side also the certain fact that even if such a view of life may satisfy individuals, it cannot be passed on to others, it is plainly incumbent on them to recognize what is involved as to their own response to the summons of the Most High.

For there is abundant reason to think that that summons has come from God attested in sublime but most appealing fashion in the evidences of His handiwork. Just as the ever-varying glories of the sunset, or of the sea tossing or slumbering beneath the radiance of the sky, are signs of His Will to adapt the pageant of natural processes to the delicate but limited sense-perceptions of mankind, so He has ordered that the Revelation He has made of His Love for us should be commended to our minds by its wondrous outgrowth in human character. That some men should be paragons of wisdom, great examples of fortitude, ministers of good things to their fellows, dauntless seekers after truth, was not unknown before the days when Christ lived and suffered in Palestine. But, after that time, what was novel and unique in the world was the proof that men could think, not little of the gifts, but nothing of themselves, the recipients: should be so rapt and uplifted with the new spiritual consciousness of Christ's Presence among them according to His word, and of all that they owed to His divine indwelling, that they forgot their own personality with its rich and glorious powers, till their fellow-men felt for the first time the spell of self-forgetfulness and the winning influence of the humble single heart, manifested in daily life before them. It was not for nothing that Polycarp and Blandina braved tortures and death rather than deny their Lord; but when one thinks of the tone of the populace in such places as Corinth, Ephesus and Rome, is there not reason to suppose that the testimony of the great unrenowned throng who showed the world what Humility really meant, was an even more potent witness to Him Who came "not in His own Name," "not to be ministered unto but to minister" and was among them "as He that doth serve"?

So it is still. Humility of character, which began with Christianity, has continued as the outcome of a sincere faith in the work of Christ, the Redeemer and Sanctifier of mankind. It may not be the most prevalent or the most striking of the evidences of Christianity, but it is the most attractive. To those who in all sincerity set the development of character before themselves as an aim incomparably more important than growth in a right religious faith, it comes with a certain reminder and a certain message too heavenly in tone to be lightly set aside. Those who assume—and they are many—that love of our brethren is all that is needed for our earthly pilgrimage, forget that wherever love of others is cold and feeble it is because egoism chills, mars and interrupts it; and the opposite of egoism is that Humility which, beginning in a sense of sin, tends in its early stages mainly towards self-depreciation, but gradually passes into the far higher quality of self-forgetfulness, as the consciousness of divine fellowship and infinite mercy waxes in the soul. Then the gift of the love of others finds the way open to the human heart, as the one grand hindrance to its entering is being removed. So the two qualities coalesce and are deeply interfused, and it is only ignorance that makes us dream of growing in the one without the other.

Hence it may be noticed that to Humility, understood as self-forgetfulness which yet allows of the highest and most vital activities, belongs the property of immortality. As in regard to love, heaven is inconceivable without it. Prophecy and faith and hope we can feel will fade away; but love, and with love its inseparable constituent, Humility, will abide. It is like that which Spenser sang in his praise of human beauty—

> But that fair lamp from whose celestial ray
> The light proceeds which kindleth lovers' fire,
> Shall never be extinguished or decay.
> But when the vital spirits do expire
> Unto her native planet shall retire:
> For it is heavenly born and cannot die
> Being a parcel of the purest sky.

There is much that is most unexpected about all human

virtue. Whenever it is manifested it seems that so much has been endured for so very slight or uncertain a gain to the man himself. Especially is this true of the virtues which have developed under the influence of Christianity. In earlier days, and among primitive peoples the statement is less clearly true. The old Roman conception of Virtus, the manly type of bravery, chiefly physical, formed a necessary ingredient in the character which tended to hold communities together in presence of assaults from without. The ἀστυνόμοι ὀργαί[1] of Sophocles were likewise appreciated in Greece, and a large measure of neighbourliness was clearly recognized, if not consistently practised, in Palestine in the times of the Kings. Virtues of this sort secured an end which a common mind could understand, the stability of the fatherland. But after the religion of Christ had had time to leaven the thoughts of divers nations it is no longer so. Within a certain circle of people, virtuous achievement of the highest kind as shown in anticipation of Christianity by a Jeremiah, or a Socrates, assumes a new character. The demand on the individual becomes more searching and severe, and the benefits secured become less and less tangible, less easily defined, more outside the horizon of the " plain man " ; and yet when each instance comes to be reviewed, it is inevitably recognized as something precious to humanity, savouring not of the things of men but of the things of God ; and it appears that this account of virtue is true in proportion as the result of virtuous action is not gainful in the ordinary sense of the word.

Thus there is a mystery of goodness which is being

[1] " The moods which mould a state." Jebb's translation of *Soph. Ant.*

constantly reasserted, renewed in manifold types as the years pass. It is true of much of what we think of as lovingkindness; true also of such devotion to duty as that portrayed in Browning's "Grammarian's Funeral"; true again of the missionary zeal commemorated in a thousand records of Christian endeavour. But it is most undeniably true of that which is not so much an achievement as a savour of action, viz. the self-forgetfulness in thought, word and deed preached and practised by Jesus Christ on such a scale, and with such an infinite attractiveness and unsearchable power, that the recognition of its beauty has been perpetuated in an increasing degree ever since among the foremost nations of the earth. Something has happened which has stolen the strength of the, apparently, mightiest influence ruling individual human lives, namely, egoism. The suppression, or ignoring, of self is the trait of the highest character which most requires explanation. Self is insistent, clamorous in its demands, imperious; but more than that, it is supremely interesting, and the interest of it, the more it is annihilated in the individual owner of the Self, prevails the more among onlookers and friends. Often, during at least one stage in its growth, it has taken the form of self-depreciation. But that is not of its essence, or rather is not one of the characteristics of it which wins the human heart. True unselfishness is the mark of something far nobler and truer than the depreciation of that which, after all, is the work of Almighty God.

The question of the genesis of this peculiar quality has been the theme of the preceding pages. The facts which stand out as requiring explanation are as follows: The group of qualities which we include ordinarily in the word Humility, and of which the highest is the forgetfulness of self such as has been considered, have been to some extent and in a certain fashion described and actually practised by the Jewish singers and prophets. Among the Greeks prior to Christianity there is no teaching of these virtues powerful and spontaneous enough to lift men's ethical ideal; perhaps only in Plato's writings there are a few passages which may be said to touch on truths so high that, if meditated on, they would encourage the virtue of Humility. This is because the writer now and then partakes of the Jewish prophetical spirit, so that Augustine was inclined to the belief that he was acquainted with the Hebrew Bible.[1] In short, Plato shows that just where he is able to present some of the truth of God's attributes of Wisdom and Power he utters things which give men a certain effective stimulus of a spiritual kind. It is a stimulus towards contemplating the highest conceivable form of Being in which the mystery of human endowment receives its fulfilment and every lofty aspiration which falls within the circle of the qualities of Wisdom and Power its explanation. But even Plato understood very little about Agape—the love which transcends passion—and herein lies the simplest answer, from the human side, to the question why this noble Greek teacher failed to develop among his followers that group of virtuous qualities which appeared with some suddenness and were generally recognized after the foundation of the Christian Church.

But this last statement is still open to an apparent objection. It may be urged that in the Jewish Scriptures we have indications of humility, self-abnegation, self-abasement, and so forth, quite as complete as those given by the New Testament; or (if that estimate be chal-

[1] Cf. Illingworth's *Divine Transcendence*, p. 166.

lenged) complete enough to dispute the claim made for Christianity as the creator of this virtue or, at any rate, of man's recognition of it. The story of Abraham obeying the call, as he conceived it, to sacrifice his only son; the abasement of David after his great sin; the wonderful utterance of the patriarch Job after the revelation of God's power had been vouchsafed to him; these and many other instances will occur to the reader. There should be added to them the recurring instances of the recognition that self-assertion against God was the cause of downfall: Aaron, Pharaoh, Saul, and many of the kings. Then we have to include the matchless sayings in the Psalms, breathing the very purest spirit of humility, resignation, trust in God; in short, all the Godward temper which comprises all the group of virtues under discussion. Lastly there are many sublime passages in the Prophets instinct with the same tone: the teaching of the supremacy of God over the mightiest of the world-powers such as Sennacherib;[1] the divine control of such a ruler as Cyrus[2] and the fate of proud nations that have fancied themselves secure in their haughtiness and the greatness of their dominion; such as Assyria, Babylon and Tyre. In tones of triumphant conviction and unsurpassed beauty of eloquence, and with a breadth of view ranging over all the known record of human history, these ancient seers proclaimed, in its manifold aspects, the majesty of the Most High and the littleness of man "whose breath is in his nostrils." In powerful corroboration of these utterances we have the record of human submission to the divine will in the story of Jeremiah, to say nothing of the many martyrdoms reviewed in the well-known chapter of the Epistle to the Hebrews.[3] In what sense

[1] 2 Kings xix. [2] Is. xliv., xlv. [3] Heb. xi.

can it be truly said that Humility, or the recognition of it, was due to Christianity alone?

The first answer to be given to this question would be as follows:—Just as the lofty teaching of Plato issued in Aristotle's portrait of his ideal man from which the plainest symptoms of humility are wanting, so the sublime insistence of the Old Testament writers on man's duty of submission to God failed to prevent the development of Pharisaism—that singular growth from which were absent not so much the plainest symptoms of humility as its inward essence and all that we mean by its spirit; and if, as has been said, it is inconceivable that Julius Cæsar or Alexander the Great could have uttered the great passage in the Epistle to the Philippians [1] it is hardly more conceivable that a true Pharisee could have understood it.

In other words, the characteristic of ineffectuality which belongs to Plato's message, and which is so baffling and so distressing to any lover of humanity, is found also to belong to the doctrines of Priest, Psalmist and Prophet of the Hebrews. Not, of course, to the same degree. The teaching of the Old Covenant was far clearer, more piercing, vastly more positive than that of the Greek sage; but, more than that, it was far more powerfully corroborated by lives that were lived and deaths that were died. The greatest and most moving portrait of Humility that is to be found in all pre-Christian records is that of the Servant in the second Isaiah; [2] and it has been with much probability suggested that it was inspired by the martyr-heroism of Jeremiah. Whereas in Greek or Roman history, unless it be the death of Socrates, we

[1] Phil. ii. 1–17. Cf. Miss Wordsworth's *Onward Steps*, p. 3.
[2] Ch. liii.

have not a single picture of conduct which could be described as self-forgetful surrender to a cause nobler than that of martial patriotism; and the time comes to every nation when such patriotism lacks a field for its exercise. If, then, the inadequacy of Hebrew teaching was a fact, in spite of its being supported and invigorated by the examples of many heroes, to what may we ascribe the achievement of Christianity: its power to create a new ideal which has affected the ordinary view taken by average men and women in any Christian country, as to what real beauty of character is?

Now bearing in mind the strangeness of the phenomenon that has to be explained—the general recognition of a type of character which is opposed to deep and universal human instincts—we are met *at first sight* by the difficulty that the work of Christ resembles that of His forerunners in its aim and spirit, but differs from them in that He was one and they were many; and yet that He achieved a revolution in human ethics which they only succeeded—as far as others were concerned—in indicating. As far as conduct goes, there was something so sublime about the story of Jeremiah that we should expect to find a proportionate influence exercised on human ideals, proportionate that is to the influence of Christ. But there is no evidence to warrant any such inference. The Jews gathered the bodies of the slain prophets into sumptuous sepulchres, but the homage they paid to the martyrs did not mean any deep acceptance of their spirit. The noblest features of the Christian character were either not exhibited by their votaries or, if they were, they were not appreciated. But when the time came, we find that Christ illuminated human life with a new conception of goodness. His immediate forerunner, the

Baptist, was a shining and splendid instance of self-forgetfulness and self-abnegation; but yet we feel that even if he had been able to exhibit that example without the inspiration of the nearness of Jesus, it would not have been taken into men's minds and bosoms any more than that of Jeremiah or Ezekiel. Indeed, the passage in which it is so finely portrayed for us [1] gives the impression that it could not have been written except by one who had learned from the Lord's lips and example, under the Spirit's direction, what self-abnegation meant. The contemporary attitude towards the Baptist—as the Synoptists show, with their singular power of reproducing an atmosphere of feeling which had passed away —gave no more promise than did that of the contemporaries of Isaiah, of any final acceptance of his message. This the later Evangelist notes with precision, "He was a burning and a shining light: and ye were willing *for a season* to rejoice in His light." [2] We are still, then, seeking an answer to the question, What is the explanation of the permanence of the introduction of genuine profound humility into the group of virtues recognized among mankind?

As compared with the life of Socrates, or the teaching of Plato, the story of Jesus Christ gains, of course, immensely in the power of the sinless example and further from the ineffably winning attraction of His personality. But there is no reason to suppose that either the teaching, or the example, or the personality, or all three together, could have wrought the change in men's minds that was actually wrought, had it not been for the interpretation of His Person which established itself soon after His death and has been maintained in His Church from that

[1] John iii. 24 *sqq*. [2] John v. 35.

day. Further, I would urge that the power of maintaining this interpretation vividly and genuinely, and, still more, the power to see what it involves, is the direct outcome of the gift of Pentecost and cannot be otherwise explained.

To amplify at any length these statements, after what has been said, is needless. We have Christ's warrant for considering the nature of a child, the characteristic of childhood which is most typical and most lovely, as a guide to the solution of questions such as these. He told us that childlikeness is the note of those who enter the Kingdom of heaven. He left us to put together what we know of children, namely, that the development and vigour of all that is most beautiful in them depends on their knowledge of their parent's love and that, during the precious years when a child is most truly a child, there is a strong tendency to something like self-surrender, which is added to the natural self-forgetfulness, if only the manifestation of that love has been blended with that of wisdom, strength, justice, godliness. In proportion as these elements enter into home-life, we find children showing the very qualities included in the term Humility. If they are physically vigorous their activities are symptoms of their upward striving towards the ideal set before them. The utmost reward they look for is a word of approval; while, if they are now and again disobedient, the slightest token of the parents' love being wounded brings them instantly to show the grief they feel, without the least attempt at excusing the fault or reluctance to put their feelings into words. In all this they exhibit the opposite of the self-assertive wilfulness which is incompatible with Humility; and if we add to it the self-forgetfulness which, besides being natural, is the outcome of their constantly pressing towards something higher than themselves which is not themselves, but which they instinctively feel they can appropriate and win; then we have the tone of character which in its wondrous freshness and charm is almost entirely restricted to childhood, but which, in its deeper elements, is found among those who have passed through storm and conflict, but have learnt that the revelation of the Love of God can restore something of the long-forgotten vision.

For humility is recognized not by children only, but by grown men, who first lost "*novitas ea florea mundi*" owing to the insistence of the idea of a personal self as childhood passed into adolescence. Thus it is not enough to see what the revelation of earthly parental love will do for the child whom nature equips at first with self-forgetfulness. We are brought face to face with a far greater wonder: the development of this grace in selfish adult life; the overcoming of a pervading vice of character which has been allowed free play as the years went by. How has this been brought about?

The knowledge of the Love of God for man[1] has worked the miracle. Not the recognition only of the beauty of the character of the man Jesus; because if that were all, the story of the Gospel would only be one more record of supreme goodness overborne by supreme selfishness; "one more triumph for devils, one more insult to God"; and indeed it would be the greatest of all such triumphs, the most unanswerable of all such insults. No, it is the sense of infinite Love combined with infinite Power and Wisdom, called out

[1] Tit. iii. 4.

by the knowledge that God Himself became Man, and conquered Death by enduring it.

Finally, just as there was gross and invincible misconception of the work of Isaiah, Jeremiah, and the Baptist, so there was of Christ and of His work and His teaching. But it has not prevailed in the conflict. Something happened which altered the relative power of the contending forces. Instead of the weak-hearted group of 500 followers or thereabouts, the only apparent fruit of our Lord's ministry, being the one hope of the new religion, we find 3,000 gathered into the divinely-founded Society in one day, and we gradually come to see that the three years during which the Saviour lived and worked among men, were, in one aspect at any rate, a preparation for the Pentecostal gift. In relation to our subject, this view of Christ's work is all-important. It is as if the Almighty Father tried first one help, then another, then a third, for His weak and bewildered children. He endowed His chosen people with a genius for religion and for recognizing the relation between man and God. Further, He summoned into life the piercing imagination of Xenophanes, Parmenides and Plato. The latter failed because, whether men caught the philosopher's drift or not, philosophy is powerless, without living personal example, to lift the lives of mankind. The former failed, though the sublime teaching was fortified by lives of wondrous self-surrender and unquenchable trust. The message was too lofty and human egoism too strong. When at last One came with a message of still more august import, with a summons to a self-surrender far more complete, and to a trust which no earthly distress could undermine, though again the heavenly words were illustrated by a triumph over all the subtlest forces of the world of evil: pride, egoism, love of ease, impatience at wilful blindness or chill indifference; yet once more the Ambassador from the unseen realms of life would have failed to bring His meaning home to the heart of man, had it not been that the Divine Spirit of Wisdom and Understanding, the Third Person of the Holy Trinity, Himself descended into the arena of the struggle on which angels gaze, and gives to those who seek Him the things of Jesus.

Then, and not till then, did those special graces of the Christian character which we think of under the title of Humility win acceptance and wide recognition among all nations. They needed the intervention of God to call them forth, but no sooner were they manifested by the pioneers of the Gospel, than even the pagans felt the mysterious correspondence with their deepest instincts, and owned their gentle mastery. For centuries the germ of them had been lying dominant in the human soul.

Archbishop Temple appealed to Christians thus:[1] "Let us ask ourselves what it is that really binds men together . . . where shall we find it?" and from the teachers of the Far East comes the earnest call that all thoughtful followers of the Crucified should set themselves to state with increasing clearness wherein the central message of Christianity really lies, that with undiscordant voice they may proclaim it to the expectant millions. May it not be said to lie just in the few propositions: that the Life and Death of Christ revealed once for all to men that the God Who made us, loves us infinitely; so that even sin, in some way only partly

[1] *Onward Steps*, Miss Wordsworth, p. 1.

understood, is done away with by His blood-shedding; and His mind and character are perpetuated in the Society of believers vitally and with undiminished power; because the Agent by Whom this is brought about and Who alone enables us to take in the truth so far is the Holy Spirit Himself?

EXCURSUS I

THE TEACHING AND EXAMPLE OF CHRIST

There has probably been at all times in the Christian Church a considerable number of those who are naturally drawn towards an "undogmatic" view ot Christianity, that is to say, a view which in the main represents the work of Christ and of the Church in subsequent centuries from the human side, eliminating at least by profession all that implies a definitely new revelation from God, a definite interposition by Divine Power in the normal routine of the world's history. Nebulous as such a religious creed seems to others, it may be admitted at once that many of its votaries are men of the highest character and intelligence. There is no appeal aginast them on the score of moral weakness, as if such weakness were more clearly noticeable in their case than in that of more dogmatic Christians. But it may well be that there is a special question to be asked of them which refers not, strictly, to virtuous living but to clearness and consistency of thought; and that is whether such a position is not in reality an abdication of the responsibilities laid upon us as reasonable beings, which we all agree theoretically in recognizing.

Such an abdication has been made by those who definitely refuse to make up their minds as to the Christian hypothesis concerning the work of Christ. The shallowest enquiry into that work shows it to be a fact in history of quite stupendous influence on human affairs: on man's fears, hopes and powers. As such, apart from the tremendous character of its affirmations, it comes before every one of us with an urgent claim on our best understanding and most reverent thought. That is to say, if a man is a being endowed with reason, it is hard to see how any adequate estimate of that gift is consistent with a refusal to use it on a matter so unspeakably great; so infinite in its scope, and yet so personal and individual in its message.

This affirmation appears to me to be, strictly speaking, unassailable, as long as it is admitted that such a thing as responsibility for the right use of mental gifts exists. Among those people who adopt an agnostic attitude towards Christian doctrine there are very many who are quick and ready to admit this particular responsibility, and in many departments of life they discharge it faithfully. I wish particularly to bring the challenge home to those who would go further than others in definiteness, and would willingly allow that, whatever may be said as to Christ's Person, there can be no doubt about the sublimity and power of His teaching and example.

The challenge is that they should clearly face the question how far this teaching and example remains entitled to man's reverence under the postulate that the Christian hypothesis is doubtful, or unnecessary, or untrue. More particularly, I am considering the position of those who have lately banded themselves together to promote the training of the young by moral teaching without religion.

As bearing on the question I will take some of the leading features of the Gospel teaching, and, on the assumption that Christianity was somehow stimulative of virtue, discuss whether such an effect can be attributed to Christ's work on the purely human hypothesis. It is commonly admitted that Love and Humility were first recognized as essential to virtue, to that winning attractiveness of character which is more potent by far to bring support to a Creed than any amount of logic, at the time when the work of Christ began to tell on men's minds; and the theory now under discussion is that the teaching and example in conduct and action were the causes of this result, even though they be interpreted purely from their human aspect.

A passage which claims a foremost place chronologically, as bearing directly on the subject of Humility, is the Magnificat. How are the familiar words "He hath scattered the proud in the imagination of their hearts," "He hath exalted the humble and meek" and "the rich He hath sent empty away" to be accounted for? On the traditional hypothesis the exalting tone of this sentiment expressed by the Blessed Virgin is paralleled by our Lord's words "I thank Thee, Father, Lord of Heaven and Earth, that Thou didst hide these things from the wise and prudent, and didst reveal them to babes"; spoken at a moment of great rejoicing of spirit. In both passages there is expressed the joy of one who sees clearer than before the prospect of a great deliverance, the help given to Israel, the falling of Satan from Heaven: the token of a wondrous display of God's love for man. The knowledge of the nearness of the great event enables

Mary to see that God's scheme of salvation is transcendent in the power and love which it reveals; and that in its light man's much vaunted resources and glory fade into utter insignificance. This fact in itself is no reason for joy; but only as an indication of the greatness of the divine interposition in human affairs.

Now strip off the religious colouring of the Magnificat, and what remains? There would be no way of explaining the reiterated expression of joy at the reversal of human ideals. Why should any one feel glad at the discovery that all that mankind had agreed in exalting—the proud, the mighty, the rich—were abased, scattered and put to shame, unless something immeasurably nobler and more enduring were put in its place? There would be something quite insensate in the folly of swarms of people gathering together day by day or week by week, to sing a hymn set to the finest music available, and celebrating the downfall of mankind's most prevailing hope, the utter baffling of his desire for strength and power and glory, and that the foremost nations of the earth should continue this singular pastime for 1,800 years is a fact which, without some religious explanation, would brand mankind with the stigma of lunacy. There would be nothing surprising or humiliating in men being obliged, under the stress of experience, to modify their ideas of the *summum bonum* of life as the centuries rolled on. But imagine a state of things in which a certain set of ideals, denoted by the words, rich, mighty, etc., were pronounced by a certain peasant woman in Palestine to be hollow, useless and outworn; then that for the 1,800 years following, those ideals should apparently persist in almost undiminished vigour among the very people who every seventh day repeat the glad announcement of their downfall, after having discarded the theory which first prompted the words to be uttered, and which alone makes them intelligible! If this is what is really going on, there would be no more disputable utterance to be found in any great writer than Shakespeare's well-known saying: "What a piece of work is man! how noble in reason! how infinite in faculty! . . . in apprehension how like a god!" Indeed, it would be difficult to form any idea of the purpose of the creation of beings who, endowed with faculties of thought and logic, are yet thus irresistibly impelled to violate them.

It is, however, open to any one to answer this challenge by the rejoinder that we sing or listen to the Magnificat, without attempting to yield assent to its sentiments or understand its drift, merely from old associations, or because it is in a way not unedifying to repeat the utterances of one who spoke under the influence of what she took to be inspiration nineteen centuries ago. Or it might be said that whatever the Magnificat may be it is not part of the teaching of Christ, and so lies outside our proper subject.

Some such answer as this would probably be made, so, leaving on one side the question whether it is worthy of rational beings, we pass on to some salient features in the teaching and example of Christ.

The Temptation

In spite of a great deal that must be mysterious about this event, we are bound to consider it with all possible attention since it is one of the very few incidents which apparently must have been told specially by the Saviour to His followers, else it could not have been recorded. At this point it may be convenient to say that the challenge as to the value of the Gospel lessons on the "undogmatic" hypothesis is addressed to those who, in the main, accept the authenticity of the Gospels as they stand. It is of course, always possible to take refuge in some crude theory of Gospel reconstruction, which would allow a critic to put on one side this or that passage if he found it militate against his theory. But there are many thousands of men and women who, without any knowledge of such theories, or without any wish to make any selection from the materials before us, vehemently assert their firm confidence in the ethical teaching of the Gospel, and it is only fair to suppose that they mean by the phrase the lessons to be drawn from the records handed down.

Moreover, without attempting to be precise as to anything mysterious, and even if the narrative is simplified as much as possible, the ethical teaching of this story may be distinctly set forth. The Saviour is represented in a state approaching starvation directly after His Baptism, and with His mind evidently dwelling on the work which He was to do. Conscious of power to supply His physical wants with a fiat of His own He refused to do so. Why? If He had succumbed to the inclination, He would have done no harm to any one, and the imminent collapse of His plans would have been averted. Now I submit that on the Christian hypothesis, and guided by the teaching of the New Testament, we can find an answer to this question, but on any other hypothesis we cannot. If Christ was the Son of God, we can faintly imagine His trust in God being so complete that He could not for one moment place His reliance on any other source of strength, not even on His own power over Nature; but He was bound to act absolutely and always by the divine dictation, and to assert before mankind the power of a life lived wholly on spiritual principles, and therefore free from anxiety as to physical needs, regulated ever from above, never by consideration as to earthly necessities. This is plainly to make the personal relation between man and God paramount over material claims, no matter how insistent they be; and in thousands of lives lived since, the same power of action in very varying degrees has been manifested by Christ's followers.

But on the hypothesis that Christ was merely human, that God does not make His will in these matters clear to His children, where are we? In all the three temptations, the choice was, as far as we can see, between what people call mysticism and common sense. Judged by common sense, the Saviour's decision is wholly unintelligible. It would have been expedient for Him to throw Himself frankly and fully on the one thing left to a man whose personal trust in God is denied him, viz. his ascendency over his fellow-men. And not only expedient, but necessary if He was to do anything at all in the world; for on the "moral" or "undogmatic" interpretation of the passage there was nothing else whatever for any one to trust to. In short, by the Christian interpretation the story is the record of a supreme but quite characteristic act of self-forgetfulness (or *ignoring* of self, according to Christ's own words), because of the undimmed clearness with which He perceived His relation to His Personal but unseen Father. On the other theory, that "dogma" may be wisely omitted from our explanations of the Gospel story, Christ renounced all reliance on the power of His own self to win ascendency over men, and shape the course of human history as He wished, with nothing whatever to put in its place. His conduct was either a sublime self-committal to a Person, or a colossal and meaningless blunder. A Christian would say that He displayed the only form of self-reliance which is ever found to be unassailably strong and supreme over the baffling vicissitudes of earthly life: the committal of self to a living, present God. The moralist on the other hand cannot conceive of any self-reliance as being other than what the words denote, reliance on self. Such reliance has often been remarkably successful in making a great stir among men and doing things whicih have been subsequently found to be useful; but be it what it may, it is the outcome of a theory of man's being, which was contradicted by Christ quite invariably, and with the plainest emphasis in the incident of the Temptation in the Wilderness.

The Finding in the Temple

On the human hypothesis this event was an act of disobedience on the part of a boy of twelve explained by Him in meaningless language. Yet one would be loth to believe that artists, poets and commentators have all been wrong in regarding the incident as a precious illumination of the Saviour's boyhood, and a striking anticipation of His mature life on earth. The mere moralist's view is that, on His first visit to the Temple since His infancy, not only was He profoundly impressed by what He saw and heard around Him, but for the first time found an opportunity of learning from the best instructed men in Jerusalem at an age when He could understand their teaching; and the fascination of this early lesson made Him forget His parents' wishes. In this there is nothing mystical. But the words with which He answers His mother's remonstrance show us that already He was beginning to interpret His work on earth as a definite commission from God His Father. As such, the excuse is sublime, but only on the assumption that it was not an outburst of misguided enthusiasm, harmless in a child, but certain to grow into something dangerous later. It was sublime if it was true; that is, if He felt the premonition that He was to fulfil the yearning aspirations of the Old Testament and complete what the long line of prophets had centuries before foretold; and if this premonition was definitely imparted to Him by the Eternal God. But let us be quite clear about the matter. If the young Jesus only imagined that God had called Him to some special work, too wonderful to be interfered with for a moment even by the claims of home life, then He was the victim of a tragic hallucination, and the more intensely He believed in it the more certain was He to meet His end in utter ignominy as a fanatic. Again, it seems that a choice must be made between the two views. In the human view, if a boy disregards his parents' orders and pleads a commission from the Almighty, he is either a mere dreamer or an egoist of the most pronounced type, hardly sane. Clearly there is nothing so far in the mere human Example of Christ to inspire His followers to the self-forgetfulness of "true and laudable service."

THE SERMON ON THE MOUNT

The versions of this discourse as given by St. Matthew and St. Luke, though differing in some important respects, agree completely in one characteristic. The precepts recorded are sublime and inspiring if the view they suggest of God the Father is true. But if for any reason the relation between man and God, which they assume, is ignored or put out of account, the exhortation is wholly valueless except as a specimen of successful popular oratory. Take the passage which, perhaps more than any, has touched our imaginations, the appeal to men not to be absorbed in anxiety about material needs, supported by the instances of the lilies of the field and the birds. If, as it may be suspected is often thought, the words merely touch some common emotions and are not meant to be pondered on and practised, then they are far less effective than much poetry and rhetoric which has been poured out on similar topics for many centuries. But if they are to be taken as *enforcing a truth,* viz. that God is continuously and personally concerned with each one of us having enough to live on, they at once become sublime, because they are so vastly above all prudential maxims of ordinary common talk. But it follows that the truth indicated of God's Love and Fatherhood comes to us from Christ's teaching with a tremendous urgency and an authority which it would be insanity to resist. To trust God in times of severe trial is no doubt hard. But to try to do so is reasonable, when once it is admitted that Christ's words express a truth. On the other hand, to hold that they do express a truth, and then to affirm that the truth may be ignored in the view of life to which we give ourselves, is a gross violation of the reasoning faculty with which we have been endowed. The affirmation about God is either like a tinkling cymbal, or it is the greatest truth by far of any to which men have ever tried to give their minds.

Another great passage is concerned with sincerity of conduct: the warning against practising what is considered virtue for the sake of men's applause. Here again it is open to us to recognize the grand underlying principle of Godwardness of service; or if we choose to believe that that principle is unimportant, or dubious, or untrue, then we are bound to show some reason for admiring the teaching; in other words to indicate some rival principle on which the precepts are based, as large and comprehensive as the one we have rejected. This is not easy to do. "Take heed that ye do not your alms before men." On the theory that God is our Personal Father who stirs our sluggish hearts to service in gratitude for His revelation of Love to all mankind, it is intelligible that the performance of service, either to Him or our fellow-men, rendered in order to win applause is an act of disloyalty to God; a symptom of the double-mindedness condemned by St. James, and of the attempt to serve God and Mammon which Christ has pronounced an impossibility. It is indisputable that the singleness of heart which Christians believe to be essentially acceptable to God as it certainly is to men, the sinking of self, the victory over inclination, the shrinking from self-assertion, all of which virtues appeared in vigour, and were for the first time recognized, in the early Church, are based upon the principle of a certain relation between God and man; and that this relation, if it is a fact at all, is a fact before which all others, unconnected with it, sink into insignificance, and the ignoring of which is a treason to our own minds. If it is ignored, what are we to make of the warnings against seeking men's praise? A very common view is that the reward of public favour, titles, promotion, etc., is necessary to induce men to overcome their native sluggishness of purpose and mental indolence. Is it not far better that we should give alms mainly because we enjoy the commendation which we reap therefrom, than not give at all? The approval of good and wise people, one would think, is a reward worth working for. This is common sense as it is called; but unfortunately, it contradicts flatly the precepts of Christ. Those of us who hold that Christ had the power of revealing the true relation in which we stand to God, are perfectly prepared to explain how this is. The one thing we cannot explain is how admiration for the precepts is consistent with a denial of the principle on which they rest, and with a loyal adhesion to the opposite principle which contradicts them.

The Preaching of Repentance

One of the most prominent characteristics of Christ's teaching was the continual assertion of the need for man of a new view of life and its meaning. Here is a claim which cannot be gainsaid without definite denial of the truth of His conception of the deepest things. But unfortunately we have most inadequately translated the word *μετανοία*, which expresses this new view, by the narrower word Repentance, and therefore, some of the greatest sayings have failed of their effect. Yet the well-known words "except ye be converted," etc., express the same.

injunction as μετανοεῖτε, and it certainly is most astonishing how prevailing is the power of ignoring this command and of continuing to profess loyalty to the Gospel teaching. "Change your view of life permanently." Such is the plain rendering of μετανοεῖτε. But change from what? Clearly from the conventional view which dominated men's minds at that time, not only in respect of ethical principles but of all deep matters. Life is a totally different thing if Christ's teaching about the nearness of the Most High God to each one of us is true. If it is not true, then the Jews did right to put their Messiah to death, for He was then the most powerful preacher of falsehood and builder up of baseless hopes that the world has ever seen. If it is true, it is lunacy to speak of it as insignificant, and still greater lunacy to begin by denying it, and go on to profess admiration for the teaching which assumes it. If true, it furnishes us with a theory of life which has been able to produce characters so noble as to compel reverence from all who have learnt to know them. If it is either untrue or insignificant, then our only sensible course is to go on as if we had never heard of it, indulging our inclinations whatever they may be, just so far as not to incur the displeasure of our contemporaries.

The Lord's Prayer

When Christ was definitely asked by His followers to teach them how to pray, He gave them the prayer which we call after His name. It is reasonable to expect that it contains a statement, in the form of a petition, of that new view of life alluded to above. At any rate the principles assumed in the prayer can hardly be at variance with those which underlie the main lessons taught by Christ to mankind.

There is no need to travel outside the simple structure of the petition; that is to say the order of the clauses and the order of the words. But let us remind ourselves first of the point under discussion. The question is whether a merely moral view of Christ's teaching and example is not a wholly false view. Whether the disposition freely manifested in modern times to discard all that deals with the relation of God to man, called "dogma," does not threaten to leave nothing behind of any value at all; and is not utterly inconsistent with any fair interpretation of the teaching.

We find then that the prayer consists of separate clauses, the first five of which emphatically assume that very view of life and its issues which mankind has often found it most difficult to take, though men have been irresistibly impelled to do it homage. It is the doctrine or theory of the Fatherhood of God, and His guidance of men's lives from day to day. If this doctrine be true, then it is most reasonable to pray that man's conception of God's attributes may be holy and true. (" Hallowed be Thy Name.") Next, that the Kingdom spoken of by Christ should be speedily established. (" Thy Kingdom come.") Next that the benignant purpose of the all-wise Creator be fulfilled by His children on earth, even as we believe it is fulfilled now by other beings in a more exalted kind of existence. (" Thy Will be done, as in heaven so on earth ; " but there is little doubt the last words are to be applied to all the preceding petitions.) Then as the part man has to play in the fulfilment of these hopes is important, since indeed it is essential that he brings them about by his action, not that they should be carried out independently of him, the prayer deals with man's primal necessities, physical (" Give us day by day our bread "), ethical (" forgive us, etc., and lead us not into temptation "), and spiritual in the distant future, but beginning now (" deliver us from evil ").

Such is the prayer Christ gave us, and it embodies with the utmost clearness that very view of life and its issues which millions of professing Christians are disposed to ignore, while declaring their reverence for the moral teaching of Christ. Let it be further noted that this pattern-life was lived by One Who habitually prayed Himself, and obviously must have used petitions breathing the same religious spirit as the Lord's Prayer. Indisputably that was the secret of His amazing power, His constancy, His utter tranquillity of spirit in the midst of unspeakable calamities, shame and ruin.[1] So that those who speak confi-

[1] It might be thought that it would be safer to attribute these characteristics of our Lord to His essential Godhead. Doubtless on such a subject great caution is needed. But we cannot be wrong in studying our Lord's life on earth with the formula in our minds " Perfect God and Perfect Man," and I am assuming the latter clause to mean that the perfection of Manhood is in its dependence on God. Man is only perfect when he is perfect in receiving ; and Christ manifested God to us by the perfectness of His receiving and appropriating the Divine Life " seen in fleshly form on earth." It is, of course, conceivable that He might have been what He was in Himself on earth, if He had never shown outwardly any sign that He was in communion with the Father ; but this would have deprived His example of all that is fundamentally essential for us to imitate.

dently of following the example of Christ are bound to have some theory as to their practice of prayer. Almost the only thing in Christ's moral example which any humble follower can at once begin to adopt is His practice of prayer. But prayer means prayer on the lines of the Lord's Prayer; that is, based throughout on the principle which we call religious: the principle of entire dependence on God's Will and trust in His Love.

Lastly, if it be said that in this prayer there is emphasis laid on a moral principle, that of mercifulness to those who wrong us, I would ask what meaning can be attached to the idea of forgiveness of each other, unless we are prepared to annex to it the statement "even as God for Christ's sake hath forgiven" us? It is of course most difficult to put oneself at the undogmatic point of view, because one of its characteristics is to be unformulated. But if it means an indisposition to realize the divine side of such a conception as that of forgiveness, while asserting its sufficiency from the moral side only, the question must be definitely faced, On what does the duty of forgiveness rest? Doubtless the unmerciful man, if unchecked by the law of the land, might make himself a nuisance to society: but that is only if his vengeful thoughts found expression in action. Christ's teaching, however, as is well known, emphasized the deadly evil of wrong thoughts, and every one knows that we are quite as distinctly forbidden to nourish rancorous thoughts as we are to do violence to our neighbour. Now, from the moral side only, what mischief would be expected from the rancorous thoughts of a well-bred man who thoroughly understood what society demanded of him? In the twentieth century it would be odd if we were not to some extent steeped in Christian Ethics; and by this time most of us have discovered that a really forgiving man is a better companion than one who is given to vindictiveness. But that only means that the vindictive man must be very careful not to betray his feelings in an intemperate fashion. Some ways of betraying them civilized society would readily condemn; others it would approve. No one for instance would expect a social ban to be fixed on an injured person who took his revenge in uttering polished and amusing sarcasms against his injurer. Yet such conduct would indicate a heart completely alien from the Christian spirit. But that is because Christian ethics do not regard the opinion of human society as its first concern, but the relation between society and God Who allowed it to be formed. Some may aver that they descry a reason for recommending the forgiving spirit to young people, servants, rustics and so forth, but is it a reason which would for a single moment elevate this duty to the level on which the Saviour has placed it? There is no conceivable doubt that He based it on the revelation of divine Love which He Himself made to mankind, and to base it on anything else whatever, such as the welfare of the community, or the amenities of social life, is to be more disloyal to His teaching than if we disregarded the duty altogether. Why? Because if it were frankly and consistently disregarded we should at least know after a time that the atmosphere in which we move had been poisoned. But if it is partially and externally obeyed from any reason but the right one, we are stupid enough to believe that we secure the social advantages, such as they are, from a mundane motive. In other words we break two commandments at once; the Sixth in thought, and the First as well, because we set up some earthly god in place of our Father Who is in Heaven.

The Death of Christ

It might be supposed that enough instances had been brought forward at least to illustrate our contention, viz. that a really high estimate of our Lord's teaching and example presupposes the Christian "dogmatic" interpretation of the Gospel story. But the matter cannot be fairly dealt with without some consideration of the Passion and Death of the Saviour.

We pass now to that part of the story which gives us the example at its very highest; that is to say it is the climax of all His conduct through the three years of the Ministry. It represents more clearly than any other part of Christ's public career the depth of the antagonism which He aroused and the heroic strength with which He faced it. Hitherto we have been concerned mainly with the teaching. Now we have to make up our minds as to the example of One Who so lived before the public that after three years He was put to death by the religious leaders of the day.

In this connexion an important fact is that the shameful close was deliberately provoked. Now, to all those who persuade themselves that the human view of Christ is sufficient and satisfying, or that the "mystic" interpretation is superfluous, or that outside the moral teaching and moral virtue exhibited to men every other question as to His Being and Personality is out of our depth, the following question seems not easy to answer. If the example of Christ is of supreme value to mankind, on the human or "undogmatic" hypothesis, how are we to explain that He threw away His life after so paltry a period of ministering to His generation as three years? (The question assumes that He knew what He was about, and deliberately brought death on Himself. If, however, it is thought possible to believe that He did so unwittingly, the form of question would only be slightly altered, and the argument would remain.) Nothing is more admirable and impressive than the example of a martyr who dies for an idea. But what should we say of One Who courted death, foresaw it, foretold it, made no effort to shun it when the crisis came, and all the time was possessed with no idea clear enough for His admirers to discern when He had passed away? The difficulty, however, is even greater than this. On the hypothesis we are discussing Christ must have known that the power of His teaching and the loftiness of His moral example were the chief means whereby He could hope to elevate mankind. Was He then more likely to succeed if He restricted His efforts to three years or allowed them to extend over thirty? If He faced this question and answered it in the negative, what becomes of His judgment? If He answered it in the affirmative, how can His conduct be approved?

In short, if the earthly life of Jesus of Nazareth is rated as something precious and unique because it affords to us a supreme example of goodness, wisdom, courage and love, we ought to explain why He cut it so short. The contention of Christians is that no explanation is possible which does not draw upon religious conceptions: i.e. postulate such divine interposition in human affairs as must be, if true, a fact of overwhelming importance to any one who can think at all. But such interposition is, by the moralists' theory of the Gospel, either denied, or more strangely still, treated as insignificant.

Let us imagine an answer to this challenge as complete as we can make it.

The figure of Jesus in history is that of One Who saw with wonderful insight into the shallowness and sham of the popular religion of the time, and exposed its worthlessness with unsparing emphasis. Moreover, He was gifted with such healing powers and such force of oratory, that His influence over the people might have been unbounded; but His ethical position was too high for them; and by consistent and most impressive self-denial He put away from Himself all the glittering delights of fame and conquest, and preached a religion so pure and lofty that it has remained the greatest inspiration ever given to mankind; but the line He adopted made His early death inevitable. Doubtless there was in a character so noble much that we should rightly term divine; but to define what the Person of Christ was, is plainly an overtaxing of human powers of thought and savours of irreverence: moreover it is needless.

It is possible that any one ready to subscribe to some such statement as this would assent to an educational programme which professed to teach Christ's moral example and no more of what is ordinarily called the Gospel. But the objections to the statement are very serious. It swerves away from the very central question of interest and importance. "What was the pure and lofty religion which brought Jesus of Nazareth to martyrdom and an immortality of fame?" If we profess to reverence His teaching we ought to rate highly what He taught, and the first thing to do is to see what it was. Likewise, if we call ourselves followers of His example, we ought to be clear in our minds whether His death was pure fanaticism, i.e. the heroism of a visionary, or something undergone for the sake of truth itself. If the latter, let us press towards the truth. If the former, let us look for our moral example elsewhere.

Now as soon as we admit that Christ preached an ethical code too high for the Jews to understand, or a religion which has been a source of strength and comfort to mankind ever since, it is impossible to attempt to put into words what that religion was without entering on topics which moralists at the present day relegate to the realm of the superfluous. It is open to any non-Christian to do this if he likes, without plainly contradicting his own principles; but it is not consistent with any sincere loyalty to Christ as an example, to recognize that He taught a religion too lofty for His contemporaries to understand, and at the same time to refuse to face the question, what that religion was; and the further question, whether we are not all bound to take it into our own lives and to pass it on to our children.

Supposing the moralists incline to the opinion—as certainly many do—that they cannot make up their minds on the question of Christ's claims, or on the central message for which He sacrificed His life. The time came during His Ministry when He had the opportunity of pronouncing His opinion on a very similar state of mind. He deliberately forced the Scribes and Pharisees to face the dilemma about John the Baptist "was he from heaven or of men?" and we all know that owing to the unusual mass of people in Jerusalem it was not safe for the leaders of the popular religion to say what they thought. This, however, is but an accident of the position. The important point is that as soon as they admitted that they could not say yes or no to a question concerning the greatest experience in their history, He withheld from them further light on an even greater matter. They showed themselves moral cowards, and the verdict was that, on the greatest question which could occupy mankind's attention, they were unteachable. They were without the single-mindedness which alone qualifies for advance in religious truth. But would not Christ utter some similar verdict on those who, to-day—for whatever reason—decline the Christian challenge as if it did not concern them ?

When we carefully consider the salient facts of the case the answer to this question becomes very plain. It is not possible for any Christian to give a full and adequate answer to the question propounded above, Why did Christ die ? No honest thinker could acquiesce in any statement on this subject as if it were complete. But one broad fact is undeniable. The great reason why Christ was put to death was because all that He revealed about God to men *did* concern them so closely that they felt it would alter their daily lives and upset all their pet prejudices, not in any one department of living, but in all. It was because it is always much easier to sing at intervals " God is our hope and strength " than to believe that He really loves us in spite of all our pains, suffering and sin. That is why, when the Wise Men asked the question " Where is He that is born King of the Jews ? " not only Herod was disturbed, but " all Jerusalem with him." No routine of ceremonial, no scrupulosity about custom, diet or Sabbath observance, is nearly so distasteful to man as being forced to change his whole view of the meaning of life. But that is exactly what Christ called on His followers to do. " Except ye change your view permanently " as to life and its meaning, " ye cannot enter the Kingdom ; " and as a *first* condition to fulfilling this injunction He told them again and again that they must start by believing what He said about Himself, and about the infinite Love of God for man. If they could not genuinely do this, they were to pray for the trust which such a state of mind implies. As to this, He often likened Himself to the prophets of old, who were put to death because their message penetrated so deeply, so keenly and so painfully, into the very core of the conventionalisms and selfishness of their time. After they were dead, pious hands gathered up the remains of their message, and built up the martyrs' tombs. It is always easy to honour a great man for his great sayings ; but people forget that the prophet was put to death, not because they refused to listen to his words, but because they could not bear to have them pushed home. In the eighth century that application would have meant a great upset of social life. But the application of Christ's teaching would have meant a great reversal of public opinion on all the deepest matters that mankind can conceive; for it was concerned with the fundamental relation of God to man.

The above questions constitute only a small part of the challenge to moralists which the Gospel, as we have received it, makes. Nothing has been said about some of the greatest and most signal characteristics of Christ's teaching and conduct. For instance the words "Blessed are ye when men shall persecute you" contain a paradox full of difficulty even for the "dogmatic" Christian. But, for the moralist who professes to guide his life only by the ethical teaching of Christ, it surely is a fact that not only this saying but all the Beatitudes are sheer nonsense. Our Lord's Passion and Death reveal, no doubt, how profoundly true the words are. But that is only because He exemplified throughout that drama the power of religious faith, perfect trust in a Personal Father which marvellously turned the agony into joy. When we have observed that fact, we have taken just the first step towards understanding the Lord's life on earth. But unfortunately it is exactly the step which the moralist debars himself from taking, under the idea that he is somehow loyal to his reason in doing so.

It is the same throughout. If the Beatitudes are anything better than the enthusiastic aspirations of a dreamer, they go far to explain why Christ rated all things as completely insignificant on which we habitually set the greatest store, e.g. wealth and the praise of our fellow-men. But unless the vast yet penetrating principle, drawn from the facts of the unseen world, of our relation to God is constantly kept in view and firmly held, men are perfectly justified in saying what many doubtless think, that these opening sayings of the Sermon on the Mount are not only worthless but pernicious, in that they turn upside down the picture of human life as we know it, but somehow by the beauty of their wording maintain a certain hold on man's beliefs; and not only these sayings, but the whole attitude of Christ towards the affairs of this world, progress, self-assertion, due insistence on individual rights, provision for old age and so forth, would be rightly held to be subversive of social life and intolerably unpractical, if once the religious principle is put out of reckoning.

The Christian contention, therefore, is that as the message of Jesus of Nazareth to mankind was, from start to finish, a revelation of God's relation to man—that is, a religious revelation—it is altogether idle to begin to interpret it by dealing with morals alone; and that such a way of treating the Gospel is plainly at variance with reason, on which it professes to proceed. It should further be observed that the challenge as here stated only touches on the religious claims which lie on the very threshold of any honest inquiry into the subject. For instance, in reflecting on the reasons for the Death of Christ, a Christian would hardly deign to raise such a question as Why did the Lord apparently court a death of shame? but he would unhesitatingly go on to collect the lessons which have been handed down from the earliest days of the Church, as to the deep mysteries of the Atonement and Redemption of mankind wrought by the Death and Resurrection of the Saviour, and interpreted with increasing clearness to the mind of the Church by the Holy Spirit. He would begin by realizing that a revelation from the Almighty and Eternal God must inevitably deal with truths which the human mind can only partially and gradually understand; and throughout he would shun the danger of trying to make that revelation square with the narrow range of unassisted human reason.

EXCURSUS II

THE INFLUENCE OF GREEK PHILOSOPHY

The question which demands a brief investigation is as follows: —Granting the main thesis to be sound, that somewhere between the time of Aristotle and the foundation of the Christian Church, there sprang into existence a vivid recognition of certain qualities which we now see to be absolutely essential to anything like greatness of character, can it be contended that an extra-Christian influence, such as that of Greek philosophy, was entirely, or in part, the cause of this recognition? There is no dispute nowadays as to the fact of this influence. Opinions may differ as to the time at which it began, or when it was at its height. But let us grant all that is necessary, viz. that from the greatest Greek teachers from the days of Xenophanes, Parmenides and Heracleitus down to Aristotle, the inspiration began which can be traced in its working through the subsequent ages, through Alexandrian, Roman and Byzantine time, only to be renewed in Western Europe at the Renascence, and that it is by no means exhausted yet; and this is no meagre concession; let us then consider how far it can be truly said that there was in the utterances of those wonderful minds any plain teaching as the fundamental virtue of Humility, or any encouragement to its practice.

For the limitation here indicated is plainly reasonable. If the Greek philosophers were not responsible for the result, it seems almost certain that Christianity was. At least, one grand counter-claimant must first be put out of court. Now the claim of Greek philosophy to this or any other result is only counter to Christianity if it can be shown to be justified by evidence taken *before* Christian teaching began. For instance, Seneca and M. Aurelius and Epictetus may be taken as exponents of Greek ethical teaching blended with Roman ideas; but it is far from certain that they were not affected by Christian ideas, and what is more, by the manifestation of what is called the specially Christian type of character. Therefore, they ought not to be called as witnesses to the development of pure Greek teaching. But the case would be different with a man like Cicero who was certainly influenced by Plato. If it could be shown that the Roman orator, either by teaching or example, fostered the idea of humble-mindedness among his countrymen, that aspiration after self-forgetfulness which is found and to a great extent realized in St. Paul, then there would be a *prima facie* reason for supposing that the Platonic teaching was powerful enough to make men turn away from the worldly ideal of enlightened selfishness, to the "ignoring" of self which was preached and practised by Christ.

Cicero, however, as a faithful disciple of a teacher of Humility, may be dismissed. There were certain fine points in his character, but it could not be claimed for him by his warmest admirer that he was forgetful of himself. If Aristotle's sketch of the ideal man in his Ethics may be taken as a proof of Humility being alien to the Greek philosopher's mind, so Cicero's famous letter to Lucceius [1] sets the question at rest as regards the Roman mind. When the orator found that fame in his lifetime was only going to be his in a sadly curtailed measure, he sighed all the more deeply after a posthumous renown, and took every step he could think of to secure it. Even if this estimate may seem to require some qualification, it must be remembered that we are considering Cicero not only as he was in himself, but in his qualification to be a teacher of others as to this particular virtue. The idea that this orator could possibly have been responsible for the growth either of Humility itself, or of its recognition among mankind, is nothing short of grotesque. Else it would have been necessary to have included the Porch among the possible explanations of the phenomenon under discussion.

But, before considering the effect of Greek philosophy, a word should be said as to a possible blending of the teaching of the Old Testament with that of the Aristotelian schools. Here, again, an effort should be made to see clearly the question at stake. Humility is a virtue which, however highly estimated nowadays in certain communities, must have always been, as it now is, profoundly uncongenial to the natural man, who is an egoist to the heart's core. Is it then conceivable that men like Epicurus or Chrysippus or Zeno who derived their principles from Aristotle could have been successful in planting this particular virtue in the human breast, when their great master himself not only failed to do so, but did not even try; moreover,

[1] Fam. v. 12.

saw no reason why he should try ? The truth is that to maintain that their influence in this direction could have been powerful enough to produce the result which was visible first in Jerusalem, then in Greek-speaking cities, but only after the time of Christ, would be a paradox too extravagant to be worth discussing.

Now in trying to estimate the effect of Greek philosophy in its prime on the formation of character and the encouragement of particular virtues, we may note certain tendencies in the teaching of such men as Xenophanes, Heracleitus, Socrates and Plato ; but not Artistotle, since his main principle seems to have been that the human mind could embrace and reduce to a system all forms of thought, outside of which there was nothing thinkable.[1] Even if this statement be disputed, we have enough evidence to warrant our excluding him in the Ethics alone, in the character of the high-souled or great-minded man.

In regard to the others named, it may briefly be said that if their teaching culminated in Artistotle, it is impossible to trace any effect of the kind desiderated. Plato's great successor had no clear conception of what Humility meant ; therefore whatever may have been Plato's teaching on the subject it could not have been of the creative, stimulating power required. But, on the other hand, it is interesting to note that whenever any doctrine rises above the ordinary philosophic teaching and lifts up our hearts to the Deity, it encourages a set of notions favourable to humbleness of mind, though it would be going too far to say that it could lead to anything so vital as self-forgetfulness. Thus, Xenophanes insisted on the truth that God must be something higher than anthropomorphic teaching could picture Him. In other words he would not recognize the power of the finite to conceive the infinite. So far as it goes such teaching is discouraging to man's pride. Pythagoras too " felt that some living being not an abstraction, not a creation of his own mind, must sustain his and every human polity." [2] Heracleitus, again, uttered some very stringent things about the contemptibility of the human soul ; and a fine saying of his was " Pride or Insolence should be stifled more diligently than a fire." But his notions were based not on the greatness or the nearness of the Power over man, but on the fluid condition of all phenomena. But yet it is said of him that he conceived of a " reality which he could not comprehend, which he desired should comprehend him." [3]

[1] Maurice's *Moral and Metaphysical Philosophy*, Vol. i. p. 183.
[2] Ib., p. 109. [3] Ib., p. 97.

No doubt a few other disjointed sporadic sayings might be unearthed from the remains of the early philosophers, which would indicate tendencies towards a state of opinion favourable to the recognition of Humility of character. But apart from the paucity of such utterances, the question is not only what certain teachers taught, but how far their teaching was effective in moulding the ethical conceptions of their generation; and a distinct light is shed on this question by the tone adopted by the Sophists. In spite of much divergence of opinion among scholars as to the bearing of the remarkable movement connected with the names of Gorgias, Protagoras, Prodicus and others, there would probably be few to dispute the assertion that their object was to equip young Athenian citizens with the means of acquiring power; and it would be difficult to invent any purpose or aim in life so antagonistic to the teaching of Humility. The whole atmosphere, in short, which has gathered round the name Sophist, the whole of the discussions which the interesting movement has gendered, are steeped in questions wholly alien to our subject. Men have disputed how far the Sophists were actuated by patriotism, or by desire for gain; whether the art of persuasion was or was not a dangerous toy to put into a young man's hands: whether Aristophanes was or was not out of date in denouncing them, and whether he meant what he said; but no one with any acquaintance with the tone of Athens at the end of the fifth century, B.C., would seriously propound the question whether these teachers took money for inculcating precepts favourable to the group of virtues we are considering.

Nor is it conceivable that the fascinating figure of Socrates could be taken as a landmark in the history of this subject. It may be contended, doubtless, that he left many of his youthful questioners dissatisfied with their intellectual conceptions; they must have felt themselves baffled and perturbed by a dominating personality quite free from ambition, careless of appearances, and provokingly subtle in disputations. But these are not the qualities, nor was Socrates' method the method, to encourage anything so deep as Humility of character. Supposing it be conceded that there was something either about Christ's teaching or His example, or His divine power which encouraged Humility, it is at once extremely difficult to ascribe any such result to Socrates, because there is nothing in common between the influence of the Greek who perpetually convicted his questioners of ignorance and confusion of thought, and that of Christ, Whose teaching was listened to with rapture, and Whose career caused a mighty revolution in human thought and ideals; not because His influence was destructive of old conceptions, but because He filled men's minds with a vision of the bounty of God and the grandeur of human life. If anything of an encouragement to Humility is to be discerned in Christ's work, is it possible to conceive that the genial but exasperating banter of Socrates had any similar effect? On the whole, it seems justifiable to wait for some moralist who will withhold from Christianity any of the effect undoubtedly produced, and refer it all to Socrates, before pursuing the subject any further.

In regard to Plato, much might be said bearing indirectly on the matter in hand. There are passages in this sublime writer which fill a sympathetic reader with something of the same emotion as he experiences from portions of the Second Isaiah or the Apocalypse; and I would suggest as the reason for this power, Plato's doctrine of Ideas. He conceived of true Being in a more satisfying way than the Eleatics, since he kept the objective and subjective in what must be their true relation to each other. He labours to overthrow the doctrine that the root of our knowledge is in ourselves, but recognizes that our conceptions testify to the existence of the Idea. Hence the difference between his thought and the Eleatic doctrine of True Being made him feel the awe of one who was constantly in presence of a mystery; and, through the greater part of his immortal dialogues, we can detect the reverence and humility inspired by the grandeur of his apprehension of Reality, and his utter inability to suppose, any more than St. Paul did, that he "had apprehended." Thus, his teachings has in it the essence of humble-mindedness, in that it set forth that the part of the human enquirer is not to snatch at Truth, or as he chose appropriate it, but to receive. So far as this goes, his attitude was that of the early Christians.

A few quotations will show Plato's power of waking up the idea of the godhead in man's mind, within the restricted sense above indicated.

"As the sun," he says, "is not only the author of visibility in all visible things, but of generation and nourishment and growth, . . . in like manner the good may be said to be not only the author of knowledge in all things known, but of their being an essence, and yet the good is not essence, but far exceeds essence in dignity and power." [1] Now we can perceive that teaching of this sort begins to tell on the human mind because

[1] Republic, 508, 509.

it rescues the idea of God from the Deistic theory of a First Cause, or God being simply an Originator of things, and places Him plainly before us as the Sustainer of things as well. So spiritual is the theory expounded that among "things" Plato includes man's power of knowing; God, in other words, is not only the fashioner and upholder of the earth, sea and sky, but the cause and quickener of all human understanding (τὸ τὴν ἀληθείαν πάρεχον τοῖς γιγνωσκσμένοις). He is also the arranger and controller and anything rather than "devoid of life and mind, and remaining in awful unmeaningness, an everlasting fixture"[1] but He "wished all things good and nothing bad (poor, mean) as far as possible," and hence "brought all that was visible . . . from disorder into order, thinking the latter in every way better than the former." Here there emerges the idea, rather faintly conceived, of God's beneficence, at any rate in intention. The following passage indicates Plato's view of the kinship between the human and the divine Spirit. "The most divine part of the soul is that which deals with knowledge and wisdom. . . . This then resembles the divine principle. And the man who contemplates this and so learns to know the whole divine principle would thus also best come to know himself.[2] "By acting justly and temperately you will act as is pleasing to God . . . and you will so act by contemplating the divine light."[3] "We ought to fly heavenward, and to fly thither is to become like God as far as possible, holy and just and wise." "In God is no unrighteousness at all—He is altogether righteous; and there is nothing more like Him than he of us who is the most righteous."[4]

These are great and beautiful sayings, and fill the mind with a kind of awe when one remembers the age in which they first took shape. So also "As the eye cannot turn from darkness to light without the whole body, so too, when the eye of the soul is turned round, the whole soul must be turned from the world of generation to that of being, and become able to endure the sight of being, and of the brightest and best of being—that is to say of the good. . . . And this is conversion . . . not implanting eyes, for they exist already, but giving them a right direction which they have not."[5]

Looked at more closely, such teaching is seen to be, as far as

[1] Soph. 249. See for these and other refs. Illingworth's *Divine Transcendence*, ch. ii.

[2] Alcib. i. 153. [3] Thaeaet., 176. [4] Ib., 134. [5] Rep., 518.

it goes, the kind of teaching which encourages in the learner the beginnings of Humility, in proportion as it brings the idea of God near to man. The great defect of all Greek theorizing on the Godhead is its aloofness; and this defect Plato in his best moments partially overcomes. That is to say, he draws sublime pictures, not only of a Being Who can be said truly to exist, though to do so was his main object, but of One Who busies Himself with the deepest concerns of which we have experience, namely the spiritual development of each one of us who chooses to turn to Him in trustfulness for the gift of truth. It is as if Plato's pure and illuminated soul were at times caught up into a realization of that which is to us a fundamental and essential verity of our religion, the truth that without God we can do nothing; but that all growth of mind and spirit is simply a drawing upon His life and wisdom "for our great and endless comfort." Plato gives the impression of having touched on this side of truth almost unconsciously. He set himself to discuss the nature of True Being; he occasionally was uplifted beyond his conscious quest into something of a perception of man's utter dependence on God, Who deals with him as a beneficent and all-powerful Father.

Speaking then from the psychological point of view, we may say that Plato was successful in encouraging the virtue which we see to be essential to the highest forms of human character, in proportion as he uttered the truth of man's receptivity and God's bounty. Why the insistence on this truth should be favourable to the growth of Humility, can only be understood if we conceive of Humility more as self-forgetfulness than as self-depreciation. The latter is not essential to Humility, but is found not unfrequently in combination with a spirit that is really selfish and self-absorbed; the former cannot be manifested unless there is something present to the mind which dominates and enthralls the imagination as well as convinces the reason. How is it conceivable that man should forget his own personality, even for a moment, except in presence of some display of something divine? There is nothing higher than the personality of man, except the personality of God; and the nearer a teacher can go to bringing home to men's hearts the sense of the personality of God, the more likelihood there is of man being caught up out of himself, as we say, into the contemplation of the divine.

But having said so much we are bound to recognize the immeasurable difference between the actual effect of Plato's teaching and the work of Christ; meaning by the latter expression, His teaching, His moral example, and His death and Passion as interpreted by the Church. The effect of Christ's work on human ethical standards was that of some mighty dynamic shattering the false and quickening the true ideals. Whereas of Plato we may say that, however much we may attribute to him of intellectual influence, however much we may grant that he gradually guided human thought, and that after some centuries the nett result of his teaching was favourable to the recognition of Humility; yet that all this gives him no claim whatever to have been the teacher who transformed man's conception of virtue as it was transformed between 330 B.C. and 60 A.D. Plato's influence, in spite of the moral fervour of much of his writing, was in the intellectual region taking most effect on the Christian Fathers, just as the influence of his pupil Aristotle who was in accord with his master's deepest principles, told most powerfully on the Schoolmen. But there was an element in the force which brought Humility into the forefront of human virtues, not only quickening it into actuality, translating it, that is, into the conduct of ordinary men and women, but making it into something like the very essence of goodness as men understand it; an element, I say, which operated not as a slow solvent or as a quiet, persuasive appeal to the reason, but as a life-giving power. It was a power which may be thought of as an appealing power, in that it was not coercive but persuasive, weaning man from his darling self-esteem; but it may also be thought of as a mighty and irresistible force which, carrying all before it, in a few years secured that mankind would never again fail to pay homage to Humility, however grievously they may fail in achieving it.

We may now pass on to the famous description given by Aristotle of the great-minded man. It may be prefaced by the remark that whether or not it be strictly accurate to say that it is the Greek philosopher's picture of his ideal man, it is certainly the picture of a character which he considered admirable. Therefore, if such qualities as we designate as those of humility are undeniably absent from the picture, it may safely be inferred that Aristotle had no sufficient feeling for them to be an effective preacher of humility to the men of his time.[1]

"He is thought to be great-minded who values himself highly and at the same time justly; because he that does so without grounds is foolish, and no virtuous character is foolish or sense-

[1] The passage referred to is in the fourth book of the Ethics and the translation is by Rev. D. P. Chase of Oriel.

less. Well, the character I have described is great-minded. The man who estimates himself lowly, and at the same time justly, is modest; but not great-minded, since this latter quality implies greatness, just as beauty implies a large bodily conformation, while small people are neat and well made but not beautiful. . . . Since then he justly rates himself at a high or rather at the highest possible rate, his character will have respect specially to one thing . . . now honour answers to these descriptions being the greatest of external goods. So the great-minded man bears himself as he ought in respect of honour and dishonour. . . .

"Honour then and dishonour are specially the object matter of the great-minded man; and at such as is great and given by good men, he will be pleased moderately as getting his own, or perhaps somewhat less, for no honour can be quite adequate to perfect virtue; but still he will accept this because they have nothing higher to give him. . . . He is the sort of man to do kindnesses, but he is ashamed to receive them; the former putting a man in the position of superiority, the latter in that of inferiority. . . . Such men seem likewise to remember those they have done kindnesses to, but not those from whom they have received them; because he who has received is inferior to him who has done the kindness, and our friend wishes to be superior. . . . And again, not to put himself in the way of honour, nor to go where others are the chief men; and to be remiss and dilatory except in the case of some great honour or work; and to be concerned in few things, and those great and famous."

Many readers of this extract have felt that it is a peculiarly unattractive description of a character which the writer felt to be admirable. Indeed, here and there, one is almost inclined to believe that Aristotle was deliberately humorous and indulging for once in a vein of irony; so incongruous to our notions is the grave and persistent egoism of such a passage as "he who has received is inferior to him who has done the kindness, and our friend wishes to be superior" or "but still he will accept this because they have nothing higher to give him." But on second thoughts we are deterred from attributing to this Greek thinker anything so un-Aristotelian as light, but subtle, irony, in a treatise which gives countless opportunities for such humour, but ignores them all. We are rather led to reflect that, our amazement at what we find is a measure of the change which has been wrought by Christianity in our view of each other, and in our estimate of greatness. So vast and profound is this change that even in sections of society where primitive paganism is apparently active, and instincts which it is hard to trace to any theological doctrine are allowed free play, such a character as is here described would receive a rude welcome enough. Ignorant outcasts of society, even professional criminals in modern Europe, would hardly tolerate a character so steeped in self-esteem, and certainly English schoolboys, if once the disposition of the great-minded became distinct to them, would, even in these tolerant days, take active measures to modify it. They would attempt no analysis, and would seek no excuse; but would feel that there was something in such great-mindedness which called for immediate re-adjustment. Hence we infer (1) that whatever it was in Christianity which brought into recognition the virtue of Humility and branded with ineffaceable stigma its opposite, Egoism, was powerful enough to penetrate circles of the community which either lie far from the centre of the Church's influence, or still are accustomed to exhibit the primitive temper as to their dislikes, and primitive methods of satisfying it; and (2) that this influence has been exercised so long that the obedience to it in modern civilized communities is given unconsciously, in accordance with a standard which no one any longer questions. The repellent features of Aristotle's description form a strong argument as to the greatness of the change which has been wrought in our ordinary every day estimates of goodness; and while it is fair to say that sympathy and love are both desiderated in the picture, the quality which is most glaringly conspicuous by its absence is Humility.

The failure of Aristotle in this respect may then be taken as an indication of the feebleness of the influence of both Socrates and Plato towards the subjugation of the egoism inbred in us all. Where the three greatest Greek teachers failed, it is not worth while to investigate the doctrines of their followers, the Stoics or the Epicureans, especially when we know enough of the Roman mind at the time of Cicero to be sure that their teaching had no appreciable effect upon it in this direction.

EXCURSUS III

SOME DIFFICULTIES IN PRAYER

It may have been observed that the particular attack on Prayer, put into the mouth of B (p. 65) not only assumes that the ordinary objections to "prayer for rain" hold good, but is directed with even greater vehemence against prayer for spiritual benefits, the reasons for the latter being, not scientific, but moral. In relation, not only to these difficulties, but to the rational view of prayer generally, the following simple considerations are important, but easily forgotten.

Certain bewilderments of thought are inseparable from the fact of the relation between the finite and the infinite. Our Lord in His teaching dealt with the problem in two principal ways. First He discouraged His followers from troubling their minds about matters that lay beyond their area of vision. Thus, when asked by them if there were many who should be saved, His reply was "Strive ye to enter the strait gate" (Luke xiii. 23). Again, and perhaps more significantly, when He was told of the savage cruelty of Pontius Pilate, and knowing that there was current at the time an erroneous explanation of such tragedies, He set it aside; but it is noteworthy that He gives no other. He warns His hearers against the dangerous moral view of sin to which the erroneous theory might easily give encouragement; but as to an intellectual explanation of the occurrence, seemingly permitted, of direful calamities, He says not a word (xiii. 1). This attitude towards intellectual inquiry of a certain kind is all the more striking when we remember the keen Socratic stimulus which the Saviour habitually gave to honest thought, directed towards subjects within its horizon. He often left His hearers puzzled but almost forced to put two and two together, and at least to recognize the narrowness of the prejudices to which they had been subject. All the parables were of this quality; and twice at least He seized an opportunity of directly challenging thought. Once when He showed that a familiar Psalm required a fresh interpretation (Matt. xxii. 41). Another time

He indicated with the utmost impressiveness that a refusal to use the reasoning faculty with courage and honesty was made a reason on His part for withholding further light (Mark xi. 33). Clearly there must be some very special danger in the common tendency to exercise oneself "in great matters which are too high" for us. And it may be suggested that in this subject of prayer there are questions which we may reasonably believe to be for us, at present, unanswerable; that is to say, such as require data for answering which we have not got.

Or to put it differently: man is gifted not only with a power of pursuing abstract questions for a certain way, but of knowing, or at least shrewdly guessing, that there is a limit beyond which he must not go, and yet that beyond that limit there is an answer. The power of recognizing the limit to thought, combined with a feeling that there is a beyond, is a wonderful gift, and Christ has taught us that if we neglect the power of thinking up to the limit, we suffer greatly; but that we also run a very grave risk if we try to go too far.

But more than that, He has given us a plain direction as to such difficulties, which is almost inexhaustible in its rich suggestiveness. We are to become as little children. This command is given unreservedly, and is concerned not only with such matters as the purity of childhood, its hopefulness, its dependence and so forth, but may be applied without misgiving to the subject of Prayer. Suppose we deal with the ordinary rational difficulties of Prayer, after putting ourselves as well as we can into the child-like frame of mind. What do we know of the relation between a normal young child and his father, which may help us to understand our own relation to God, in the matter of offering petitions to Him? What is that human relation when it is at its best? and does it warrant us in withholding our petitions, for reasons such as those hinted at in the text?

It is characteristic of a child who knows his father's love—and we need consider no other—to ask a good many things that can't be granted. Sometimes they are impossible; sometimes it would be bad for the child if they were granted. But the important question is, Does not the asking betray a right relation between the two, rather than the reverse? Certainly if all is right between them, the son will not yearn in silence for something he knows his father could give him. If there is openness between them, a strong desire in the child's mind will mean a petition uttered. That is the normal wholesome symptom of a right relation between father and child. We should also say that if the requests err by excess, it is far better so, than that they should err by defect.

Again, a child who trusts his father will perhaps ask for things which in an adult's view are obviously impossible; and the frequency of such petitions must vary with the child's age. But if the child is too young to know that they are impossible, we, his elders, do not blame him in the least, but recognize that, in speaking his wants freely, he is behaving as a healthy-minded child should. But if we suspected that he knew the request to be impossible, we should think the petition unnatural and foolish.

Suppose we apply these simple considerations to the great question what ought to be our practice towards God in the matter of offering petitions.

First we learn that we ought to make known our wants and not bury them in the silence of our hearts, as we are bound to do if we forget the facts of God and His nearness to us. The filial relationship requires of us to be open and candid with our unseen Father, and if we feel certain a calamity is inevitable, anyhow we can ask for strength to bear it and use it to His glory. But if, under the conviction that it must come, we keep silence, under some supposed loyalty to the laws of nature, we may be obeying some etiquette of the scientific world, but we are contradicting our own position as His children. I would further apply the canon of petitions changing with advancing knowledge to this matter. A child of five might perhaps naturally ask his father to build a bigger house for the family to live in, and to do it to-day. If genuinely made, there would be nothing wrong in this; as there would be in a child of ten. When then we are constrained to pray for rain we are asking for something about which we know very little except that we are in sore need of it. Our knowledge of meteorology is still astonishingly incomplete. We have no right, in this country at any rate, to say that a dry morrow is inevitable; and still less right have we to assume that the Creator of the universe is bound by His Own *ordinary* methods of action. I would say then, that, as long as we are plainly in a state of imperfect knowledge, we are behaving like healthy-minded trustful children if we ask God for what we want.

Further, this holds good, though we may confidently believe that in a thousand years some scientific men will be able to predict the weather in England for the morrow with certainty. Granted that increase of knowledge may change the form of the petition, does that constitute the slightest reason against our opening our hearts for the satisfaction of our needs now? The chance of any disloyalty to our reason seems very remote compared with the urgent claim made upon us to be open and outspoken with God; and if we should regard it as ridiculous to charge a child with disloyalty to his reason, why should we be so sensitive on the subject ourselves?

But at this time it can hardly be necessary to point out that the regularity of the recurrent phenomena in the universe is no proof whatever that they go on manifesting themselves in a purely mechanical fashion; that is to say, independently of mind. No one who has read Aubrey Moore's essay in Lux Mundi needs to be reminded of this. Indeed a slight acquaintance with many more accessible writings which have appeared during the last twenty years would show any honest inquirer than from the intellectual side alone there is no unanswerable case to be made against offering petitions to God.

But so much has been said on this part of the subject that I prefer to point out one or two more familiar truths connected with Christ's revelation of childhood. Suppose we grasp the main truth underlying the expression, the Immanence of God, we shall understand that a prayer for rain, for instance, is a prayer addressed to the divine Mind, asking that, that which we think of as the course of this world, may be guided in a certain direction. Assuming that the difficulties above mentioned, which may be roughly classified as scientific, are put on one side, there remains a moral or spiritual difficulty to which utterance is given in the text of this book. It is this. Granting that the Divine Being can and does guide the course of the world or universe, He is held by His worshippers to be omniscient and all-loving; how then can it be necessary for us to tell Him our wants, as if He did not know them; and if He knows them, how can we suppose that He will not satisfy them; unless of course we should be better for remaining unsatisfied, in which case our prayer had better not be made?

Perhaps in this matter, even more than in others, we should remember that we are dealing with an Infinite Being. Again, we find ourselves helped if we stick to the parallel of the child; and we realize that for a time it is well that he should look on his father as all-wise, and for all matters in which the child has any concern, as all-powerful. So far the parallel holds. Now what should we suppose if the child kept silence as to some want, from a belief that his all-wise father already knew of it and needed not to be told? Once more the answer is that such a reticence would be unnatural; it could not, in short, occur. But this is exactly the consideration which we are bound to think about; for when Christ bade us become like little children, He certainly meant normal children, whose behaviour is most childlike, in other words, natural; and so far then we may say that as this is a *practical* question, are we to ask God for our needs or not, one answer is that to decide in a negative sense would be disobedience to our Master. But we can also see why. It is not true in human life to say that the question whether a boon should be granted by a father to a child is unaffected by the petition being made or not made. Suppose a case in which it had been clearly laid down that all wants were to be made known, and entire openness was to prevail between the two, and then the father were to debate within himself whether he should give some little boon which he knew the child wanted, and was conscious of the want. Clearly, the advisability of giving it must depend on the genuineness of the child's desire for it; and under the circumstances, the rule of the house being what it is, the desire could hardly be genuine unless it were expressed; and further the desire itself is affected by being expressed. But more obviously still, the risk of over indulgence is near at hand if the child is given something which he hasn't taken the trouble to ask for, which he wants or ought to want, and perhaps doesn't really care for. So much is plain in the human relation. We have no data for saying that there are no such moral facts in the relation between us and our Heavenly Father; on the contrary, we have every reason to believe that there are.

Once more: a question casuistical of a kind is sometimes raised as follows. Suppose three people, A, B and C, are all anxious, and rightly so, to obtain a certain post which only one of them can hold. A rationalist's difficulty would surely be that the more genuine each individual's prayer, the more impossible it is to believe that God answers all genuine petitions. It is once more like the farmer on light land praying for rain, while his neighbour on heavy land prays for dry weather. How can this be reasonable or right?[1]

The difficulty in tone is not unlike that put by the Sadducees to Christ about the woman who married seven brothers. It is

[1] It is said that a boy about 12 years old, son of an eminent man, a professed Atheist, wrote to his father from school somewhat as follows:—'I am going in for the History prize, and have a good chance, tho' A and B are working hard for it too. The worst of it is, you see, they can pray for it and I mayn't: which is a beastly shame.

utterly below the level of the subject and is drawn from considerations on a lower plane of existence, and one from which spiritual considerations are almost wholly banished. It has constantly been pointed out that prayer is not *primarily* a way of securing benefits, but of bringing the human into conformity with the divine will, and that reflection on the terms used by our Lord in Gethsemane would guard any inquirer from this mistake. But perhaps the truth may be stated as follows, with regard to the supposed case of the three aspirants to the one office. To make it clear, we assume that A has genuinely petitioned God and fails in his candidature; B has not prayed, and also fails: C succeeds. Normally the result would be that B falls a victim to the bitterness of disappointment; A, though unsuccessful, is enabled by communion with God to bear his failure; C, if he has prayed too, is enabled to bear the more searching temptation of success. For prayer is a means of rising into the divine light, from which earthly things are seen in a truer proportion than before; and the burden which was felt to be crushing becomes less, because of the operation of some great sustaining power which cannot be described in words.

Thus the intellectual or rational difficulty is only serious when it is stripped of all moral and spiritual considerations, and looked at as if it had nothing to do with the emotion of love.

These remarks only deal with that part of the subject which may be illustrated by our Lord's parabolic admonition to His followers with regard to their learning again to look at life through a child's eyes. In proportion as we learn that lesson, and acquire that priceless power, the difficulties here mentioned, and all others like them, are not answered logically, though they can be, but they disappear.